SIX HOURS

Running For My Life in the Grand Canyon

A Memoir

Rick Mater

Boulevard 55 Books
Los Angeles 2022

Cover and interior layout design by Jess LaGreca, Mayfly Design

ISBN (paperback) 978-1-736-8230-3-3
ISBN (ebook) 978-1-736-8230-4-0

Printed in the United States of America

1 Running 3 Sports 3 Memoir 4 Grand Canyon 5 Baby Boomers 6 Cardiac

*This book is dedicated with love to
Jeanne Marie Blanc, Gene Paul Mater, Philip Edward Mater,
and Joshua Whitworth Wing Mater.*

And to Cassidy and Jamie, whose journey is ongoing.

CONTENTS

PART TWO: DOWN BY THE RIVER

PART THREE: THE ASCENT

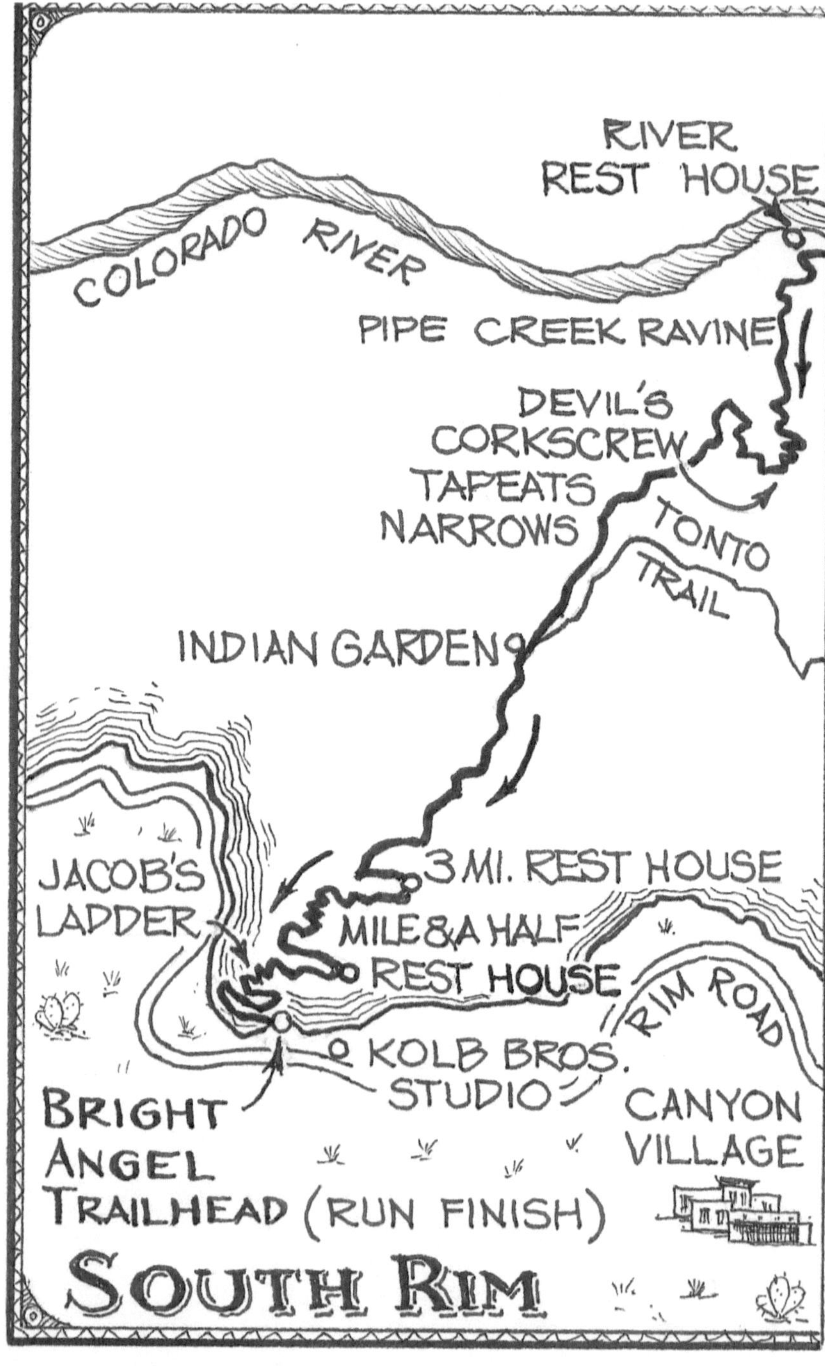

RIVER REST HOUSE
COLORADO RIVER
PIPE CREEK RAVINE
DEVIL'S CORKSCREW
TAPEATS NARROWS
TONTO TRAIL
INDIAN GARDENS
3 MI. REST HOUSE
JACOB'S LADDER
MILE & A HALF REST HOUSE
RIM ROAD
KOLB BROS. STUDIO
BRIGHT ANGEL TRAILHEAD (RUN FINISH)
CANYON VILLAGE
SOUTH RIM

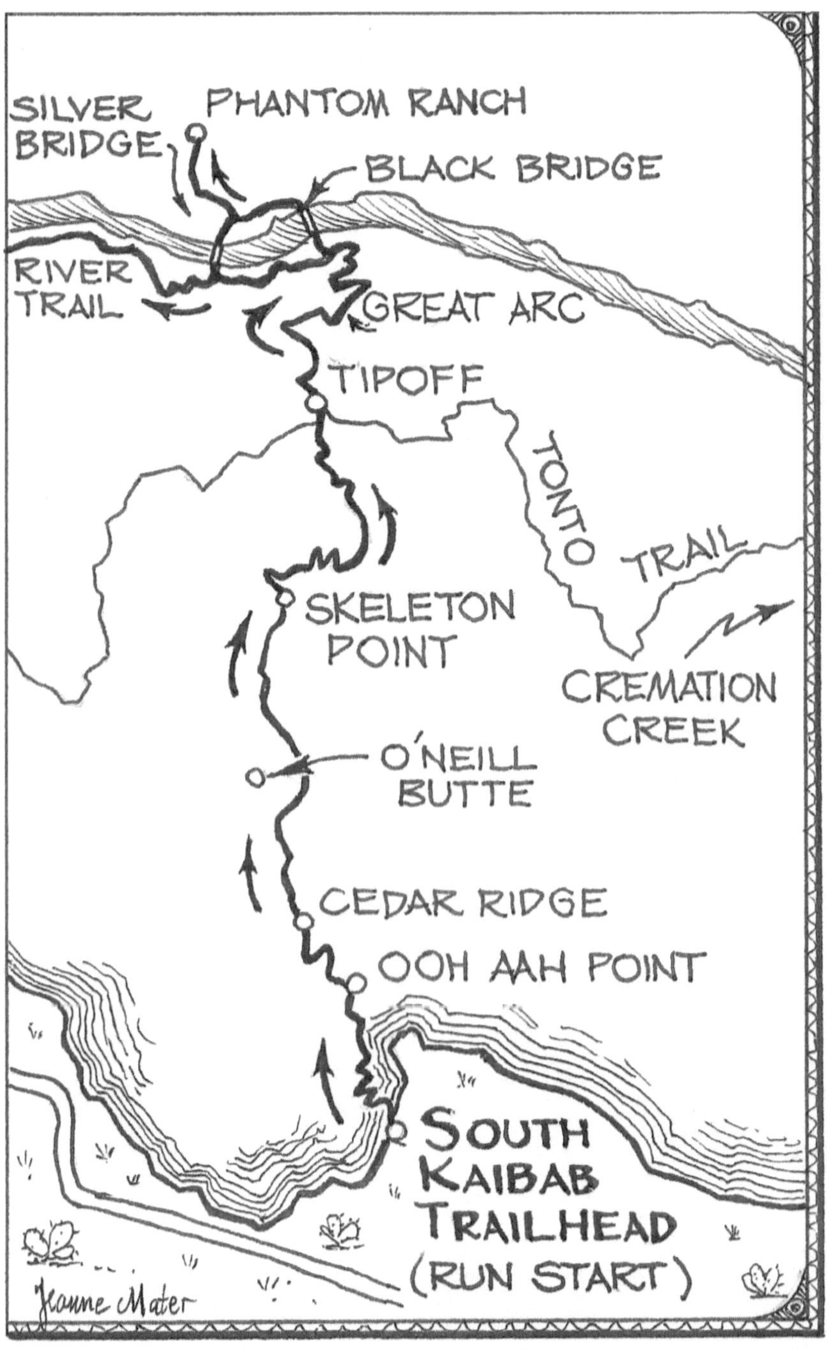

SILVER BRIDGE
PHANTOM RANCH
BLACK BRIDGE
RIVER TRAIL
GREAT ARC
TIPOFF
TONTO TRAIL
SKELETON POINT
CREMATION CREEK
O'NEILL BUTTE
CEDAR RIDGE
OOH AAH POINT
SOUTH KAIBAB TRAILHEAD (RUN START)
Jeanne Mater

GRAND CANYON, ARIZONA
SATURDAY, JUNE 2, 2012, 5:20 AM

I was running down the spine of the South Kaibab Trail at dawn, plunging seven miles into the heart of the Grand Canyon. So far so good, but given my medical history, there was the question of whether I should be doing this at all, much less alone.

Around me towered canyon walls, their red, brown, and purple hues barely illuminated in the early morning half-light. The North Rim, pine tree-crowned and distant, faced me across the multi-hued chasm, the Colorado River invisible somewhere far below.

Except I wasn't focused on majestic vistas and scenic wonders. I was watching where I put my feet. For one thing, strapped to my back was a green and black Patagonia daypack containing the awkward heft of five bottled waters. For another, I was navigating the steep descent, with the narrow trail's switchbacks, rutted rough spots, and sheer drops of hundreds of feet off the edge. As a result, I wasn't running all out. I was doing a controlled scoot down the ridgeline—entailing quick, short strides and careful foot placements.

I was closing in on Cedar Ridge, nearly a quarter of the way to the bottom and my destination: Phantom Ranch, where I would take a brief break, eat a peanut butter and honey sandwich in my daypack, strip down to my Coolibar short-sleeve top, get back on the trail, and begin the brutal ascent. I wanted to get out of the inner gorge, where the oppressive heat could suck the energy out of you and worse, well before the temperature hit the 105 degrees predicted by the National Weather Service website. I figured I could complete the 17-mile route and be standing back on the South Rim before noon, and hit my time goal. A guy I guessed to be thirty years younger than me, judging by the photos on his runner's blog, posted that he'd run the route in five hours and change.

I was going to match him.

Kathy, my wife, was back in Los Angeles and questioned the whole endeavor. Her biggest fear: at 64, with my cardiac history, I would drop dead in the Canyon and leave her behind to raise our two daughters, Cassidy and Jamie, ages 15 and 12, alone. Actually, that wasn't completely true. Kathy's biggest fear—the one that made her try to talk me out of running the Canyon today—wasn't that I would drop dead, but that I would suffer an incapacitating stroke and come home in a wheelchair, still alive. If that happened, Kathy would need to put her formidable skills as a registered nurse to work, feeding me with a spoon while a mixture of drool and bits of food dribbled down my chin, as she angrily told me. I'd be unable to walk, go to the bathroom and urinate and defecate by myself, or take a shower alone. Confined to the first floor of our house, I'd be a living reminder of the mistake she made eighteen years earlier, marrying a guy twelve years her senior with an as yet undetected medical crisis in the making.

And Kathy had a point. Thousands of people hiked the Grand Canyon each year—some even ran it. But they hadn't escaped what should have been a massive, fatal heart attack, and required an emergency angioplasty, three stents placed—a fourth stent joining them in another angioplasty just eight months ago.

I shouldn't be running at all. I should be dead.

   RICK MATER

PART ONE

THE DESCENT

CHAPTER 1

DEATH IN THE GRAND CANYON

NIGHT BEFORE THE RUN

"Hello, my name is Ken. I'll be your server this evening, sir." I glanced up at a fresh-faced young man standing expectantly at my table. He looked like a college student.

"Please don't call me 'sir,'" I said.

"Yes, sir. Oops, sorry!"

We shared a laugh.

"Can I get you something to drink?"

I perused the wine list. "I'll take this Cabernet Sauvignon by the glass," and I pointed to it on the menu.

Ken said, "Good choice. Be right back."

I glanced around the restaurant located in the surprisingly nice Best Western Premier outside the main entrance to Grand Canyon National Park. The hotel boasted an expansive lobby with a faux marble floor and bubbling fountains. The Coronado Dining Room, where I was seated, featured lavender tablecloths, color-coordinated purple cloth napkins, place settings with wine glasses, and four high-backed leather chairs to a table. Tasteful paintings of Canyon scenery hung from the walls. A nice-looking, albeit deserted bar area faced me across intervening unoccupied tables; there was a row of vacant barstools and a bartender drying glasses with a hand towel. It wasn't quite 6 PM, and just a smattering of people trickled in, the place still nearly empty, servers standing at the ready.

I was happy to have snagged a last-minute room next door at the Holiday Inn Express after my decision just days before that this was going to be the weekend of my run, preceded by the 500-mile drive from Los Angeles. I preferred to stay inside the park, but I'd been unable to garner a reservation, since it was peak season, and everything was booked.

At the Holiday Inn, I'd been given a mini-suite upgrade, which was nice. The room had a small fridge where five bottled waters cooled for tomorrow's run. On the nightstand, an alarm clock waited to be set for 3:45 AM. For distraction from my insomnia, there was a television set; several *New Yorkers* I'd brought with me to catch up on my reading; and my laptop, should I want to get some work done.

Dinner tonight would be leisurely.

My work BlackBerry vibrated its incoming alert. I unholstered it from my belt, reached into my shirt pocket, and retrieved my reading glasses. I thumb-typed my security password and took a look. Close to 40 emails. Busier than some days, not as busy as others. I'd been checking my emails periodically since early morning. It was 9 PM in New York with the time difference, and business should be quieting down soon. This being Friday, I expected things would continue that way through the weekend.

I scrolled through the messages: a production calendar for a reality series featuring the late Whitney Houston's troubled daughter

Bobbi Kristina; a *Mormon Matchmaker* reality pilot call sheet; a reminder from executive producer Josh Berman that Season Four of *Drop Dead Diva* was premiering Sunday night with guest stars Abby Lee Miller from *Dance Moms* and actress Mädchen Amick; a script for *Drop Dead Diva* Episode 412; a note from a network attorney in New York, wondering if I knew why *America's Most Wanted* was being preempted; an urgent request from a network publicist for the content rating of the steamy *Blue Lagoon* remake; roughcuts of *Dance Moms* 215 and 216, with their online links for screening; and the usual notifications from the network's scheduling department regarding last minute on-air lineup changes.

I emailed my assistant back in L.A., figuring I'd catch him before he left for the day. I asked him to please print off the *Drop Dead Diva* script and leave it on my desk. I sent a response to the network attorney in New York that *America's Most Wanted* was being pre-empted because the *Hatfields & McCoys* mini-series was following up its monster numbers on the History Channel with a run on sister network Lifetime, where I was posted.

From memory, I sent the TV-14 DLS content rating for *Blue Lagoon* and told the publicist it came from the Grand Canyon on a "day off." Then, I thumb-typed, "Hah!" The truth was, I didn't mind. The BlackBerry was the Great Liberator as far as I was concerned, not the Great Tether some griped that it was, never permitting bona fide job downtime. The BlackBerry—along with my laptop—permitted working from pretty much anywhere, allowing me to spend more time out of the office. At this point in my career, that was huge.

"Here you go," Ken said. He placed the glass of wine on the table and stood there.

I took a sip.

"How is it?"

"Very good."

"Great! Are you ready to order?"

"Sure. I'll have the filet mignon, baked potato, and the dinner salad. Italian dressing on the side."

"How would you like your steak?"

"Medium."

"Seven ounce or nine?"

"Nine," I said.

"Sour cream or butter on the baked potato?"

"Butter. How about some sour cream too?"

Soon, I was slicing through the Coronado's grilled filet mignon topped with the menu's promised tasty "bistro butter." I placed a generous portion of the juicy steak on my fork and ferried it to my mouth. Delicious! Next, I scooped up some baked potato soaking in melted butter and took another bite of the dinner roll slathered with the stuff. For a night, I ignored my conversion to the more restricted diet I'd adopted in the wake of my should-have-been-fatal cardiac emergency, eating healthier with the hope of reducing my body's seeming production of artery-clogging plaque at an alarming rate.

I'd cut down on red meat and cheese (no more wedges of Gouda, Cheddar, or Brie—well, most of the time anyway); I'd made snacks like potato chips rare and banished ice cream almost entirely. Even before my first angioplasty, I'd been eating margarine instead of butter for years and drinking non-fat milk, except for a splash of one-percent in my coffee. And I avoided fast food with rare exceptions.

"Is everything satisfactory?" Ken wanted to know.

"Yes, hits the spot." My table was next to one of the large windows that lined the back of the restaurant, with views out onto shrubbery-lined paths. An older couple moseyed along as, above them, ominous black clouds approached from the southwest across the Colorado Plateau.

I nodded towards the clouds. "The weather forecast is almost zero chance of rain tomorrow. What do you think?"

Ken peered outside. "Don't worry. It's like that a lot this time of year, but it usually doesn't mean anything."

"Well, I know there can sometimes be flashfloods in the Canyon, at least in the late summer and fall. Not so much now."

"Oh, so you're doing some hiking?" Ken asked as he picked up the empty salad plate.

"Running," I said.

Ken appeared surprised. "To Phantom Ranch and back up?"

"Yep."

"One of the other guys and me are planning on *hiking* down next week. You must be in great shape."

I could sense him wondering at my age, factoring in the baldness, the gray in the hair left along the sides, the creases lining my face.

"Would you like another glass of wine?" he asked.

"Sure."

"Back in a minute."

The threatening clouds reminded me of an old black-and-white photo the Kolb brothers took of the Canyon with lightning crackling against a backdrop of thunderheads. The Kolb brothers, Emory and Ellsworth, had loved photographing the Grand Canyon so much that, in order to finance their passion, they earned a living taking photos of tourists trundling along in mule trains or by horseback down the Bright Angel Trail. Their black-and-white photos chronicling turn-of-the-century life in the Canyon adorned the park's Visitor Center and could be found sprinkled through various historical books and articles, online and otherwise. The photos were not just of tourists, but the day-to-day activities of miners, hikers, and hunters; the early efforts to bridge the Colorado; the work blasting out trails; and the Civilian

Conservation Corps tent city at Phantom Ranch as they completed the Kaibab Trail to the North Rim in the 1930s.

After initially working out of their own tent, the brothers constructed a small combination studio and house next to the Bright Angel trailhead, with magnificent views out over the Canyon. Their headquarters was completed in 1905—the same year the grand old El Tovar Hotel and restaurant opened nearby. At the time, the Grand Canyon increasingly attracted tourists arriving on the new Santa Fe train spur, its station just a few hundred yards from the South Rim, with large adjacent pens for mules and horses. These were the beginnings of a bustling cluster of structures and services on the South Rim that today was the Canyon Village.

The Kolb brothers' building was now a cute little tourist shop still clinging precariously to a ledge on the South Rim, with the Kolb Studio sign above the door. The store was filled with CDs, posters, and various souvenirs for sale as new-age music played over the sound system. My younger daughter Jamie and I had wandered through it a year ago—my first visit to the Canyon in almost 40 years.

"Hey, Dad, why don't you get this!" Jamie said, holding up a book.

I walked over to her from perusing trail maps, guidebooks, and posters.

She handed me *Over the Edge: Death in Grand Canyon*—a bulky 500-page paperback prominently mounted on a display stand next to more copies of the book in a stack. I took in the heft of it and examined the cover. It featured the title emblazoned in lurid red and yellow over a fuzzy color photo of the Canyon and two planes colliding in mid-air; down below, a skeleton, partially clad in tattered clothing, was sprawled in the semi-arid terrain. In the middle of the carnage, a rainbow arced incongruously, and a cover blurb promised: "Gripping accounts of all known fatal mishaps in the most famous of the World's Seven Natural Wonders."

As Jamie wandered off to look for souvenirs, I browsed through the book, which detailed hundreds of lives lost in the Grand Canyon. The tally was more than 700. If you deducted 126 killed in the 1956 mid-air plane collision depicted on the cover, and another 25 lost in a similar 1986 mishap involving smaller planes—deaths that didn't truly occur on the ground in the Canyon or up on the rim—there were still approximately 550 known fatalities. Hikers, boaters, riders on horseback and mule trains killed by animal spills from trails. People getting close to the edge for photos, backing up a step too far, or dangerously clowning around for the camera, resulting in a stumble, a trip, and a fatal fall. There were the heart attacks and strokes that were on my mind, typically felling people as they hiked. People also tried to swim the frigid Colorado River and drowned. People on the trails became lost, driven to dehydration madness by thirst and 100-degree-plus temperatures. In the end, they often died alone, sometimes in some godforsaken cul-de-sac of a dry streambed during a thirst-crazed attempt to leave whatever main trail they were on and make it down to the river.

And *flashfloods*.

Flashfloods occurred due to a confluence of geography and meteorology: the North and South Rim sat on the Colorado Plateau— the second highest plateau in the world after Tibet's—at elevations as high as 8,000 to 9,000 feet. The book's co-authors—an experienced Colorado River guide, along with a physician who was the medical director for Grand Canyon National Park—informed the reader that plateaus could create their own weather. Adding to that recipe for potential trouble, Arizona received northward migrations of monsoon storms from the Gulf of Mexico and sometimes the Gulf of California, especially from mid-July through September and October.

The resulting storms could be abrupt and drop an inch or more of rain in no time. They also could be extremely localized and originate miles away from the Canyon. They were impossible to detect if you were on a trail and unable to see the horizon, only the abrupt demarcation of rim and sky above you. Compounding things, the Grand Canyon's semi-arid climate meant there were plenty of rocky, sandy slopes, often barren of sufficient vegetation and soil to absorb the rain. As a result, water flowed down into the Canyon during rainstorms, collecting from rivulets into streams, ever stronger and more dangerous, until a wall of mud and debris rushed down ravine trails and seasonal streambeds, sweeping everything before it.

Being exposed elevated ridgeline, the South Kaibab Trail, my choice for the descent, wasn't a flashflood risk. But Bright Angel Trail, for my return up to the South Rim, was a ravine trail and a whole other story, with steep canyon walls, especially from Indian Garden down through Pipe Creek to the Colorado River. The further into the Canyon, the more dangerous the funneled rain became. *Death in Grand Canyon* cautioned to be careful hiking the Canyon during times of potentially rainy weather, notably in July through September, the summer monsoon season.

As an example of just how treacherous rainstorms and their flashfloods could be, *Death in Grand Canyon* told the story of university professor Roger Clubb, 36, and his young son Roger Clubb Jr., 8. The duo hiked down the Bright Angel Trail to Indian Garden on August 3, 1963, while Roger's wife Jean and their 4-year-old son Eddie stayed behind at the El Tovar. Roger and Roger Jr. made their way down the Bright Angel switchbacks to Indian Garden, four-plus miles below, where a storm began dumping an inch-and-a-half of rain. Hikers, including the Clubbs, took shelter under the large cottonwood trees.

After the rain stopped, father and son headed back up Bright Angel. Suddenly there came the roar of a debris flow hurtling towards them. Roger Clubb realized his young son had lagged behind. While hikers scrambled uphill on either side of the trail to safety, Roger raced down ahead of the approaching mass of chest high debris. The other hikers looked on helplessly to witness father and son engulfed by the flow and swept away. Their lifeless bodies were recovered buried a few hundred yards from the point of impact.

"You going to buy the book?" Jamie wanted to know, a poster in hand.

"Don't think so," I said.

But when I returned to the Canyon a month ago to first trial hike tomorrow's 17-mile route before running it, I went back to the Kolb brothers' studio-cum-tourist-shop, purchased *Death in Grand Canyon*, and immediately began reading it cover-to-cover in my room back at the Maswick Lodge.

I absorbed the book's safety lessons. Flashflood cautions aside, the book advised: Always carry enough water and know where more is available (e.g., springs, non-seasonal creeks). Always make sure someone knows your route, especially if you're alone. (Kathy knew mine for tomorrow's run.) Start out very early in the morning, particularly during the summer months, to beat the worst of the heat. And should you run out of water, *never ever* leave the main trail for a shortcut, especially to try to get down to the Colorado, no matter how thirsty you got.

I placed my steak knife on the table. In between bites of my forbidden feast, I sent out half-joking emails to my younger brother and a couple friends, using my second BlackBerry—my personal one—announcing my run tomorrow and referencing my meal as "The Last Supper."

Ken the waiter approached.

"How is everything?" he asked.

I looked up at him. He was so eager and young.

"Delicious," I said.

"Do you need anything else?"

"Thanks, I'm good." Before he could leave, I said, "Summer job?"

"Yes. I go to the University of Arizona."

"What's your major?"

"Accounting."

"So, you're going to be a CPA?"

"Steady income guaranteed."

"You don't sound happy about it."

Ken appeared to hesitate. He glanced at a couple who had just sat down, but a female server headed over.

"It's my father's idea."

"What's yours?"

"Well, I'm in a band."

"What instrument?"

"Guitar. And I sing lead on some of the songs and do most of the writing. We won a contest recently in Phoenix. We're supposed to get a free demo session as part of the prize." His face lit up as he said this, speaking faster with enthusiasm. "But it's a long shot making it in the music business," he added.

"What year are you?"

"Junior in September."

"Well, if you don't mind my two cents, get the degree, and then go for it in music."

"You mean, don't take a CPA job?"

"Right. Maybe move to L.A."

Ken looked like he was considering it, but then he said, "I don't know, my dad—"

"*Go for it! Don't look back*," I said, with an intensity that surprised me. More calmly, I continued, "You only go around once in life. You don't want to look back at age 60 and say, 'I wonder what would have happened if I'd stuck with the band thing?' You can always return to accounting."

"Gee, thanks!" he said. "It's good to hear another take on it from somebody else my dad's age."

Older, I suspected.

"I better get back to the other tables."

As he headed off, I watched him go. He moved efficiently, talking with one of the waitresses while keeping an eye on the tables. I took him to be a winner in the genetic roll of the dice—at least for now. About 5' 10," almost three inches taller than myself, good-looking, with dark hair and an almost pretty-boy face. Nose not too prominent, complexion good, jawline and chin strong. He appeared to be athletic, trim in the hips, his face friendly, open, innocent still.

I wondered what would become of him. Go for the making-it-in-music dream? Achieve it against the extravagant odds? Succeed where I'd failed in my own years-ago artist-management fling with the music business. Or instead, would he marry young, have kids, work as a gainfully employed CPA, maybe eventually move up the company ladder?

Would he turn out in the end to have the wrong genes when it came to DNA pre-determined illness and death: cancer, cardiac, diabetes, or something else? Once you got past the usual genetic ease of the teen years and 20s and 30s, there was the starting-to-get-risky 40s and the first of the shockingly young heart attacks among those you knew or knew of, and in the obituaries reported online, in the press, and on TV.

The ever more deadly 50s, cancer showing up with greater frequency, along with other life-threatening maladies, and yet more heart attacks.

The 60s, when all bets were off.

It all went by so fast. Suddenly, you were just *there*, wishing for a reset button. A chance to do it all over again. Maybe do some things differently this time. Maybe a lot of things. An alternate set of choices and decisions, especially the early ones made so young that you couldn't anticipate the outcome and the impact on the chain of events that would become your life story.

I considered my Canyon challenge tomorrow. I would never be the same runner that I used to be. I'd lost up to 10% of my blood circulation from an unaddressed circumflex artery blockage that, five years ago, my cardiologist judged not to be worth the risk of its own separate angioplasty. That was in addition to the should have been fatal complete blockage of my left anterior descending artery and having three stents placed. There was the heart attack I'd suffered while on a run that precipitated the angioplasty, leaving permanent coronary muscle damage in its wake.

But I'd resolved my life wasn't going to come to a standstill because of my medical issues. I wasn't going to go gently into that good night. That meant forging ahead with my run, regardless of the risks, the wishes of the family, and the advice of my cardiologist.

If my number was to come up tomorrow, running the Grand Canyon was a fine way to go out and as good a place as any—better than most—to die. And if so, I was going to go out satiated. Besides, the doctor who did my first angioplasty told me, "Sometimes these things are just genetic"—regardless of proper diet, exercise, not smoking, not being overweight. So, what was the point of observing a strict diet anyway, especially tonight?

I speared the final piece of steak with my fork, scooped up the last of the baked potato, and polished off the second glass of cabernet. I looked around the room. There was more than a smattering of diners now, the place filling up.

Ken returned with the dessert menu and picked up the plates.

"I'll take the apple pie," I said, scanning the menu. "With a scoop of vanilla ice cream."

"How about some whipped cream?"

"Sure, why not."

CHAPTER 2

A RACE WITHOUT MILE MARKERS

GRAND CANYON, ARIZONA
SATURDAY 3:35 AM

I leapt out of bed like a shot at 3:35 AM, startled awake by the staccato beeping of the alarm clock after I'd finally fallen asleep for an hour and a half. I went about things with the precision of a military mission, first hitting the switch on the Black and Decker single-cup coffee maker I'd brought from home. The coffee failed to induce its usual pre-run bowel movement, probably because I'd backed up my plumbing by stuffing myself last night. That made me uneasy. I always had a bowel movement before a race—and what was today but a race without competitors and mile markers?

Once, before the San Francisco Marathon, I had to find a spot in the bushes on the Marin side of the Golden Gate Bridge to do my last-minute business due to long lines at the Port-a-Potties. I used the wadded-up toilet paper that I always kept in the waistband of my running shorts for races and long training runs. Today,

I was glad I had a partial roll of just-in-case toilet paper at the bottom of my daypack.

I skipped a shower, as it made no sense. In a few hours, I would be dripping in sweat. But I took a quick shave to avoid appearing unduly grungy as the day wore on. Then, I headed out of the bathroom to the kitchen, wearing only my Jockey briefs—snug and perfect for running; they provided lots of support, so I didn't bounce around in an unwanted state of "free-balling."

I took out a half-loaf of whole wheat I'd brought, along with a serrated knife and small jars of peanut butter and honey. I sawed off four slices of bread, made two sandwiches, and sealed them in Baggies. Retrieving the five chilled bottles of water from the mini-fridge, I placed them in the daypack, along with the sandwiches, where they joined a pair of sunglasses, the detailed Grand Canyon trail map I'd found at a bookstore in L.A., a small flashlight, a power bar, and the toilet paper. I may have been cavalier about dying in the Canyon in my assessment over dinner, but as a practical matter, I was going to do everything in my power to avoid that outcome—beyond undertaking this run in the first place.

I stashed my personal BlackBerry and my cell phone into a small zip pocket at the top of the daypack, which gave me two different services: T-Mobile and AT&T. Neither had reception inside the Canyon, but sometimes, one worked better at the rim, and I wanted to be able to call Kathy as soon as I emerged.

I walked out into the mini-suite's sitting area, placed a bare foot on the coffee table, and squeezed the tube of DuraScreen SPF 30 sunblock Kathy ordered for the family by the carton. I applied the white goop generously to my arms, nose, neck, and ears, and rubbed some on my forehead and the exposed scalp on the top of my head. My calves and thighs received a coating, front and back, with quick strokes.

My legs had lost most of their hair, as if aging in reverse, becoming strangely youthful looking, almost pre-adolescent with their bare, smooth skin. My calves still looked good, I thought—maybe even better without hair. My ass, on the other hand, had betrayed me. I'd recently stood naked and sideways in front of the full-length mirror in the master bedroom hallway at home, my head twisted around, as I checked out a bug bite that had overstayed its itchy welcome. I was shocked instead to focus on little folds of saggy skin collecting at the base of each once-firm butt cheek.

Really? When the hell had this happened? I'd always just assumed, without much thinking about it, that this part of my anatomy would remain unchanged. You got used to appearing to the world a certain way. Your face and the rest of the front of you displayed a gradual process of aging, confronted daily in the mirror. While you may or may not have made peace with it, you were at least—maybe painfully—aware of your hair loss over time, the lines forming on your face, plus those three or four hairs that had started sprouting on the tip of your nose in your 40s, necessitating regular shaving. There was also teeth-discoloration, and whether it was worth the effort of whitening strips and pursuing any other cosmetic solutions. My dentist had a thriving business installing veneers: fake perfect teeth affixed in front of your real ones, and quite popular in Hollywood. I'd passed on her offer.

I put on my gray, long-sleeved Asics stretch top, retrieving it and the rest of my running gear from my *Buffy the Vampire Slayer* travel bag. The carry-all tote was a souvenir from my tenure at the Warner Bros.' WB Network, which was the high point of my television career. I'd joined the risky broadcast start-up in 1995, leaving a secure position at NBC for a promotion to Vice President at Warner Bros., which later became Senior Vice President.

At the WB, I built a network Standards and Practices department from scratch, overseeing a program lineup that eventually included iconic hit shows, like *Dawson's Creek*, *Felicity*, *Charmed*, *Everwood*, *Smallville*, *7th Heaven*, and the aforementioned *Buffy the Vampire Slayer*. If I had a career legacy, likely it was helping to facilitate the WB's groundbreaking teen dramas, with their edgy language and sexually frank dialogue. There was also the first-ever gay male romantic kiss on broadcast television in *Dawson's Creek*, between two just-graduated high school seniors, and an early rare lesbian kiss in *Buffy*.

Over the stretch-top, I added the sleek, white Coolibar UOF 50 short-sleeved T-shirt Kathy had special-ordered online to protect me from the blistering Canyon sun. I shoved the matching white Coolibar cap, with its French Legionnaire desert-style neck protector, into the daypack. For now, I would wear my regular running cap with "Phidippides" across the front, purchased from the Encino store of the same name.

Next, I slipped on my old khaki walking shorts. I'd owned the shorts for so many years that I no longer had any idea when and where I'd purchased them. Just that the label read, "Polo by Ralph Lauren"—ironically fancy, considering their current use. I appreciated the functionality and durability of the khakis, and they made the most sense for the sections of the ascent that would require power-hiking rather than running. The khakis had pockets that couldn't be beat: two on either side at the waist, unusually deep and spacious. There were also two good-sized rear snap pockets and a bonus snap pocket in front on the left leg, where I placed my driver's license and my medical-alert notification, both claimed from my wallet. "Stent Implant Card" was printed across the medical alert. It unfolded into four rectangles, each a little smaller than a credit card, with bar codes that could be scanned for vertical lines of data containing angioplasty details, including the position of the stents, should that information be needed if I was to suffer a medical emergency on my run.

My wallet also held a typed list of daily meds with their doses and my doctor's contact information. The reverse side noted my medication allergies: Morphine and Vicodin. I added the piece of paper to the bonus snap pocket. I would take my wallet with me but leave it in the trunk of the car rather than carry it, cumbersome, in a back pocket or my daypack. I took out an emergency $20 bill and put it in a pocket, not even sure exactly why.

I'd considered doing the Canyon in all-out running mode—a CamelBak hydration system strapped to my back, with its dangling tube for sucking out up to three quarts of water; lightweight nylon runner's shorts; and low-cut running socks. And if I'd done this 30 years earlier, I would have used that gear. In the end, I decided to go with a daypack instead, because of its ability to carry seemingly anything I could possibly need, and my functional khakis. I opted to wear thick, white cotton crew socks for more cushioning, tossing an extra pair in my daypack should I end up with a waterlogged slip of the foot while crisscrossing Pipe Creek on its rocks.

What to do about taking my daily cocktail of medications? The 325 milligrams of aspirin I'd be on the rest of my life to help prevent blood clotting (the familiar white pill); the 75 mgs of Plavix to thin my blood (a light chartreuse pill); Verapamil, 200 mgs to help manage blood pressure (a large orange and red capsule); Crestor, 20 mgs—recently upped from 10 mgs—to further improve my cholesterol numbers (another chartreuse pill); and 7.5 mgs of Altace for additional blood pressure control—three small orange capsules. In Los Angeles, I ran early in the morning on an empty stomach, waiting to take my meds until after breakfast. Today wouldn't be any different. I would hold off until I came out of the Canyon. I didn't know what my cardiologist, Doctor Stephens, would have to say about that.

I took a seat on the couch in the sitting area, daypack at my feet, and laced up the old pair of Asics that would soon be kicking up dust on the South Kaibab trail. They could make for tricky footing with their worn treads, especially on the Great Arc's slippery, sandy surface. The Asics were dirty white, with hard-to-make-out gray, black, and gold stripe adornments, and red trim at the ankles and near the heels; a "Made in China" tag was stitched onto the underside of the tongue. It was hard to believe they'd ever been new. I wished I could simply go out and buy another couple of pairs. But running-shoe companies had an annoying practice of introducing new models seemingly every few months. Old favorites disappeared as shoes became more colorful and flashier, their heels a half-inch thick, sometimes more, with cushioned insole inserts. Everything was science-based foot technology touted as "improved," "performance enhancing," "revolutionary!"

When I was a miler in high school, we ran in primitive leather track shoes around a cinder oval full of pits and ruts, especially on the curves. I managed to break five minutes nonetheless, with several finishes in the upper four-minute range. The only thing I had back then that was performance-enhancing were the arch supports that I slipped inside my shoes to keep my flat feet from hurting. A podiatrist had taken a plaster of Paris model of my foot and made metal arch supports covered in thin flesh-colored leather. I ran on them as a member of the cross-country team my junior year at Munich American High School in Germany. I lived there from age 11 to 17 with my family, because my father worked as the News Director for Radio Free Europe, which broadcast to the Iron Curtain countries.

I still used the arch supports as a miler my senior year of high school in New Jersey, and when I lettered in cross-country my freshman year of college. The leather on the inserts had split by then, the metal shining through. Sometimes, I wasn't sure if I still really needed them or if they were some kind of talisman. Not to mention, they were an uncomfortably hard surface inside my shoes.

Running shoes now came with built-in arch supports in the form of cushioned inserts. But I still had difficulty finding shoes to fit my feet, which were not only flat but wide as well. Maybe I should have replaced my worn Asics and purchased some new trail runners for today. But better to run in tried and true, broken-in shoes than attempt to break in a pair of stiff new trail runners at this late date and deal with whatever resulting new-shoe foot issues could ensue.

I took a quick, final look around the room. The adrenalin was starting to build. In less than an hour, I would

Running cross country
in college

be running the Canyon. I hoisted the daypack by one strap slung over my shoulder and headed out, flipping around the "Do Not Disturb" sign, locking the door behind me, and walking out to the parking lot in the pre-dawn darkness. Already it was hinting at a warmer day than expected. The car's dashboard temperature gauge read upper 40s, rather than the predicted low 40s, which could signal the difference between temperatures in the 70s versus 80s for the return ascent.

It had been in the 80s at the South Rim when I'd arrived the day before, despite the 7,250-foot elevation. After checking in, I'd headed over to Mather Point, where the tourists gathered, many of them speaking in foreign languages and taking pictures. I gazed down from the rim railing and could see the South Kaibab's dramatic ridgeline descent visible far below and just to the east. The SK appeared even more formidable from a distance, the trail precariously strung along the ridgeline, with steep drop-offs, as it precipitously snaked its way to the bottom. All I could think was, "*Am I actually about to attempt this?*"

CHAPTER 3

IT EXPIRES WHEN YOU DO

I drove out of the Holiday Inn parking lot, past the cluster of hotels and gas stations. After the end of the commercial strip, I would arrive at the park entrance in a mile, my senior pass at the ready.

A year earlier, when I'd brought Jamie to the Canyon, we'd pulled up at the park entrance with its rustic log motif after our drive from Los Angeles. I picked a lane from one of the four choices and drove under the wooden archway. As I rolled down my window to pay the admission fee, the park ranger manning the booth gave me the once-over.

"Are you 62 or older?"

I was taken off-guard. People generally took me for somewhere in my 50s—or so I thought. Late 50s, but 50s all the same. The ranger, who appeared close to my own age and wore a nametag that said "Ron," was blowing a hole in my comforting theory. I decided to make a joke out of it for the benefit of my daughter and to cover my awkward surprise. With a hand held in front of my mouth, I cough-joke answered: "Sixty-three." In the seat next to me, Jamie laughed heartily at the sight of her father being busted for his age.

"Then, you're eligible for the senior pass," Ranger Ron said. "Gets you into all the national parks free. There's a one-time $10 fee."

I'd never taken advantage of a senior discount for anything. If I'd been alone, the decision would have been easy: No, thanks. But I'd never hear the end of it from Jamie who would tell Kathy. The teasing would be merciless.

"What's the price without it?" I said, stalling. Ranger Ron pointed to a posting just off to the side: $25 per car.

"Okay, I guess sign me up," I said, reaching for my wallet. "How long is it good for?"

"It expires when you do," Ranger Ron answered. Jamie got a big kick out of that, laughing harder beside me.

"I'll need to see your driver's license," Ranger Ron said.

I handed him my license along with a ten. After a moment, he handed my license back to me along with a piece of plastic the size of a credit card and adorned with orange cactus flowers in bloom. Up one side, it read "Senior Pass" in capital letters, and along the bottom, there was a nine-digit number.

"You need to sign it on the back," Ranger Ron said.

"Will do," I answered as we pulled away, my brand-new senior pass in hand. Jamie gleefully repeated, *"It expires when you do!"* as if it was the funniest thing ever. I suspected her laughter was a release for her fear that I could die from my cardiac problems and leave her fatherless.

This morning, as I headed to the park entrance in the pre-dawn darkness, I missed my bubbly travel companion. Jamie was back in Los Angeles at school with her older sister. The day before, I'd confirmed with a ranger that the park entrance would be open at 4 AM. Now, as I drove up, I was surprised to find the multiple lanes coned down to a single available one. I slowed and pulled up at the lone booth, only to discover it was unmanned. Apparently, your reward for early arrival at the Grand Canyon was free admission. Or else somebody had missed their shift.

I picked up speed and drove past the deserted booth, continuing the several miles through semi-arid scrub and conifer woods that awaited you once inside the park. There was no indication—even if it was broad daylight—of what was up ahead. The plateau landscape was bland and unexceptional, until you reached the Canyon rim and witnessed the astounding sight that opened up in front of you.

As I drove, I kept an eye out for the small, wandering herds of deer and the occasional elk until I reached the vast, mostly empty Visitor Center parking lot. I found a spot on the outermost perimeter of the concentric rings of spaces, where it would be easiest to locate my car. Things would be far more crowded by the afternoon, when I took the shuttle back from the Bright Angel trailhead.

I got out of the car, grabbed my daypack, put my wallet in the trunk, and noticed a bus up ahead that was departing the parking lot. Damn. Had I missed my ride to the South Kaibab? I hustled over to the pickup point. There, I encountered a young guy and a girl together, along with several other people in hiking boots and daypacks, and in the case of the young couple, large backpacks, hiking poles at the ready.

"That wasn't the SK shuttle, was it?" I asked.

"I think it's a special early-morning hiker's bus," the young guy said.

"I wished I'd known about that option," I said.

"I think that's ours pulling in now." He nodded at the vehicle as it made the turn into the parking lot. More hikers came scurrying over from their cars as the white shuttle headed our way and pulled to a stop. We trooped inside, took our seats, and waited as the additional people arrived, until there were perhaps ten of us. After several minutes, the bus departed, doors closing, the noise echoing inside as the engine started up. There was just a hint of sunrise to the east.

The shuttle travelled the curves of the rim road—also known as Desert View Drive—that skirted the Canyon. The route took us through more of the semi-arid forest of ponderosa pines, gaps of ground between them reflecting the limited rainfall and the elevation. My daypack sat on the floor in front of me as I anticipated the day ahead, finally here.

TRANS-CANYON PIPELINE

Two days earlier, on Thursday, May 31st, the Trans-Canyon Pipeline ruptured a half-mile above Cottonwood Campground below the North Rim. The break washed out 45 feet of North Kaibab Trail and resulted in the closure of a one-mile section between Roaring Springs and the Cottonwood Campground. This was the third pipeline rupture in just over a week. There were two instances on Friday a week and a day ago when the pipeline broke just south of Phantom Ranch and also at the bottom of Bright Angel Trail near the River Trail juncture. The break near the ranch had just been fixed, and the one on Bright Angel Trail was due to be repaired in 24 hours, according to the Canyon website.

Constructed in the late 1960s, the Trans-Canyon Pipeline—15 miles of six-inch aluminum pipe carrying 500,000 gallons daily—originated at Roaring Springs, where a natural torrent of water spewed from a cliffside 3,500 feet below the North Rim. The pipeline first fed down to Phantom Ranch, then up the other side of the Canyon to the Indian Garden pumping station. From there, it travelled to the South Rim tanks, where it serviced the needs of the restaurants, lodges, and other businesses, as well as supplied the spigots on the Bright Angle Trail at Indian Garden and the Three Mile and Mile and a Half Rest Houses.

The pipeline was the artery that aided the battle against dehydration—especially in the summer—and was the lifeblood of the Canyon. Before the pipeline, hikers had to carry all their own water, or use the stream at Indian Garden and, likewise, Bright Angel Creek at Phantom Ranch. Breaks in the pipeline were nothing new. Portions of it were exposed to the elements and showed wear. A major flashflood in 1995 raised the depth of Bright Angel Creek from its typical foot or two to 15 feet and washed away the lower North Kaibab Trail and the Trans-Canyon pipeline. Water service wasn't restored to the South Rim for two and a half months. It took 85 trucks ferrying water daily to keep everything supplied. Due to the aging pipeline, there were major breaks anywhere from five to 30 times a year.

Today, the pipeline rupture up on the North Kaibab was still active. Hikers who planned on coming down the NK to Phantom Ranch had to instead hike down the Bright Angel or SK on the other side of the Canyon. All rim-to-rim hikes were off, no matter the weeks and months of planning and anticipation. The expectation was the North Kaibab would re-open in a week.

I hadn't sought to check the state of the Trans-Canyon Pipeline this morning. If there was a new rupture, I didn't want to know. Nor did I want to know if the pipeline still had issues on my route from Phantom Ranch to the South Rim. I was carrying the five bottled waters in my daypack, rather than traveling lighter and banking on refills. Worst-case scenario, I figured my water would get me through the run. I was going down early, it was still cool out, and I would need minimal water on the descent. I wasn't about to change my plans unless a ranger blocked my way with the authority to turn me around at the South Kaibab trailhead.

CHAPTER 4

COULD YOU RUN THE BOSTON MARATHON?

The shuttle arrived at the Yaki Point Road turnoff—a mile and a half east of the Visitor Center parking lot—where a metal crossbar blocked the way. But shuttles were permitted to go around it, using the unblocked exit lane. The barrier was erected in the 1990s to discourage day hikes down the South Kaibab by ill-prepared tourists and avoid problems similar to those on the Bright Angel Trail with the resulting rescues, near misses, and deaths. The South Kaibab was, in fact, far more dangerous for unwary tourists than Bright Angel. There was no water available on the SK; virtually the whole route was sun-exposed ridgeline.

If it was early enough, you could have someone drive you, and with no one yet around, skirt the barrier and drop you off at the SK trailhead. Also, some limited parking spaces were available if you had a special permit reserved for overnight campers in the Canyon and you displayed it on your windshield. Or you could snag one of the few parking spaces to be found along the rim road.

The shuttle carrying us made the left turn, drove around the barrier, and continued along Yaki Point Road. After a few hundred yards, it took another left and pulled to a stop. I disembarked while the young couple carrying their backpacks, sleeping bags, and hiking poles wrestled with their full-on camping gear before they followed me off.

Everything appeared normal regarding any new trail closures. The shuttle busses were running after all, and there were no rangers in sight. To my right, two Port-a-Potties stood side-by-side, with a line of waiting people who had been on the hiker's bus. Further off to the right, there was a small bathroom building that also had a line.

"Well, have a great hike," I said to the young couple from the shuttle.

"You, too," the guy said. "Hope you break six hours," the girl added. She was young and athletic looking, with blond hair and a friendly face. The two of them appeared well matched, and for a moment, I was envious of their youth and that they were doing this together. Kathy had been clear about having no desire to visit the Grand Canyon, much less hike it. Running it wasn't in the realm of consideration—no matter that she was an athlete herself as a Tae Kwan Do blackbelt, and running was a part of her Dojang's training.

"You and me both," I said.

They headed over to get in line at the Port-a-Potties. I skipped the line. I had that partial roll of toilet paper in my daypack, and I wanted to get running before there were even more hikers from the bus out on the trail ahead of me, creating a logjam.

I walked the short, winding, paved path to the rim. Dawn was breaking. The sky was cloudless. The air was crisp with the promise of adventure. Server Ken was right. There would be no rain.

It was just light enough that I didn't need to use my flashlight. I reached the display boards at the trailhead with their information about the Canyon, miles to destinations, and "No Dogs" and please-carry-out-your-trash rules, plus a brown wooden sign:

"Danger! Warning! Do not attempt to hike from the canyon rim to the river and back in one day. Each year hikers suffer serious illness or death from exhaustion."

Underneath, it was repeated in French, German, and what I took to be Japanese. Next to the warning was a primitive rendering of a guy in shorts and a T-shirt, a hand to his brow, standing against an outline backdrop of the Canyon. "Warning," in white letters against red, hung over his head.

I'd seen the sign before, of course—most recently on my practice hike to the river and back up a month earlier. The same warning was posted at the Bright Angel trailhead. There was an additional sign at Bright Angel that had grabbed my eye and tugged at my heart. That sign challenged, "Could You Run the Boston Marathon?" Below was a color photo of Margaret Bradley, fresh-faced and trim in her red racing singlet and black shorts, running the Boston Marathon. The sign continued:

"Margaret Bradley could. This 24-year-old runner finished the 2004 Boston Marathon in a little more than three hours. Margaret, a superb athlete and a gifted medical student, was a remarkable person."

Bradley completed the Marathon's 26.2 miles in a damn good time of 3:04:54 (three hours, four minutes, and fifty-four seconds). The year she ran Boston, the temperature hit an unusually hot 85 degrees. Over 1,000 runners required medical attention, but not Bradley. She completed the race just five minutes off her marathon personal record, no matter the heat, and finished in 31st place out of 10,000 female runners. In fact, she led the Greater Boston Track Club to the team victory with her pace of seven minutes a mile. The year before, she broke three hours in the Chicago

Marathon with a 2:58:52. The young runner, a graduate of the University of Chicago, was considering working towards the 2008 Olympic Trials while she attended medical school. She was known by her friends for her offbeat wit and was an accomplished classical violinist. A whole life was ahead of her, full of challenges, achievement, goals, potential, and promise.

Under her photo was: "1979-2004."

Margaret Bradley's story was the longest and most detailed of all the accounts in *Death in Grand Canyon*. On July 8, 2004, Bradley and a 20-something male friend, Ryan, decided to go for a run on the little-traveled Grandview Trail, located a few miles to the east of the South Kaibab trailhead. The duo eyeballed their route on a map beforehand and estimated the distance at 15 miles. No problem, especially for Bradley, coming off the Boston Marathon a few months before. But they were wrong. The distance they were going to run was actually 28 miles. Still very doable for Bradley under the right conditions: enough water and reasonable temperatures.

Bradley and Ryan drove to the Grand Canyon from Flagstaff, Arizona, where he lived, a distance of just over 60 miles, and parked near Grandview Point. Bradley had every reason to be confident in her abilities that day. Sometime after 8:00 AM, several hours *after* daybreak, she and Ryan began their descent down the rugged Grandview Trail.

The temperature already was about 80 degrees on the South Rim. There were none of the groups of hikers that populated the South Kaibab Trail on a typical summer morning. Or the tourists and day hikers encountered as you made your way up or down the Bright Angel Trail. In fact, on some days the Grandview Trail had no hikers—much less runners—at all.

The duo planned to take a left when they hit the Tonto Trail and run along the Tonto Platform parallel to the Colorado River gorge until they reached the junction with the South Kaibab. There they would turn left and make the tough ascent to the trailhead where I was now standing.

Bradley carried two liters of water—roughly two quarts—and wore a fanny pack containing two power bars and an apple. Ryan carried a little more: four liters, or just over a gallon. Neither runner had a map, a flashlight, or headlamp. *No one else knew where the two were headed or their anticipated finish time.* And neither of them had done the route before. Bradley had never been in the Grand Canyon. Ryan had done some hiking once on the Grandview, but that had been years ago. Even then, he hadn't been all the way down to the Tonto Trail, which would make up the lion's share of their run. They weren't starting out at dawn before the temperature began its inevitable rise, and they were running the Canyon at the hottest time of the year.

Still, they weren't going all the way into the gorge itself to face the most extreme temperatures, the Tonto Trail being about 1,200 feet above the river. But the Tonto, like the South Kaibab Trail, was sun-exposed and largely treeless, with almost no water in its streams during the summer.

On the way down, the Grandview Trail did a Y split at Horseshoe Mesa, before it reached the Tonto. The spur on the right hit a dead end. The spur on the left was a rough, non-maintained trail constructed in the 1890s, improving an old Native American route so miners could ferry ore up to the rim by mule from the Last Chance Mine on the mesa. Bradley and Ryan made the correct turn left at the fork, kept going, made it to the Tonto Trail, hooked left, and began to run west.

By 1:00 PM, Bradley was out of water, and so was Ryan. They were 15 miles into the route and would have already finished if they'd calculated the distance correctly. Instead, they were wondering why they hadn't hit the South Kaibab Trail yet. Because of the extreme heat, they decided to take a break for a couple of hours at Boulder Creek, which, while it ran with water for much of the year, was dry in July. Unbeknownst to the two runners, water had in fact been available five miles behind them, either up or down Grapevine Creek—just not where they crossed it.

Ryan was in worse shape than Bradley, so she decided to go on alone. They had to be close to the South Kaibab, she figured. But in fact, it was another ten twisting miles of sun-exposed Tonto Platform. Bradley told Ryan that when she hit the SK she would head downhill to the river instead of going uphill to the South Rim. It was easier, quicker, and at the Phantom Ranch Ranger Station, she could get help.

Now in a race for survival, Margaret Bradley ran along the Tonto under a brutal sun, with temperatures over 100 degrees and no water. Ryan began to follow her, walking, until darkness fell. Without a flashlight, he decided to spend the night on the Tonto Trail. The next morning, he resumed his trek, crossing dry Cremation Creek, 21.7 miles from the Grandview trailhead. Finally, he hit the SK, 24 miles from their start. He found an emergency National Park Service phone in its wooden box with a sign that you could use it to call for help from rangers on foot or for a rescue helicopter.

The phone wasn't working.

Ryan started shouting for help. A female U.S. Geological Survey team employee hiking the trail at 6:30 AM spotted him. She had a satellite phone with her and called for assistance. A ranger steered her to an emergency water cache. Ryan never said anything to the Good Samaritan about Bradley. He would later say he assumed she was at Phantom Ranch. Ryan drank the emergency water and consumed energy gel packets.

The woman accompanied Ryan up the tough, steep, sun-exposed South Kaibab. On the way, he mentioned Margaret Bradley to a guide with a group of hikers heading down, in case they should encounter her. But he didn't say anything about her potentially dire straits. Perhaps his judgment was clouded by dehydration. Or he was so in awe of Bradley's abilities that he couldn't imagine her not succeeding. He wouldn't have expected her to leave the Tonto Trail, so when he didn't encounter her, it was natural for him to assume that she'd made it to Phantom Ranch. Garbled communications followed. Twelve hours later, Ryan and the woman finally reached the South Rim. She drove him to Flagstaff, and once home, he went to sleep.

Bradley's family called the Flagstaff Police Department at about 1 PM the next day to report her missing. Finally, 40 hours after Bradley and Ryan separated, a serious search got underway. On July 10th at approximately 2 PM, a helicopter flying over their route saw something in Cremation Creek below the Tonto Trail. Dehydrated and desperate, Bradley had tried to make her way down to the Colorado River, not realizing she was just three miles short of reaching the South Kaibab Trail. She'd become trapped on the edge of a steep, dry 130-foot waterfall above the Colorado, where she could neither continue down nor make it back up. Margaret Bradley laid her head down on her fanny pack, curled up in a fetal position, and died—but not immediately. The time of death placed her still alive when Ryan crossed Cremation Creek and also when he met the woman who aided him on the SK. Had Bradley remained on the Tonto Trail, Ryan would have come across her.

Bradley's stunned Boston and Chicago teammates attended her funeral in Falmouth, Massachusetts. A prize in her name was established to pay the way of a young female marathoner in Chicago's Universal Sole Club (Bradley had been a member) or the Greater Boston Track Club, to run in the either city's marathon.

In the 20-plus miles of Grandview and Tonto trails, there is no record of Bradley and Ryan encountering a single person. *The Grand Canyon is visited by six million people a year, but less than 10% go below the rim.* **And** once you get away from the two most popular trails—the South Kaibab and Bright Angel—you are literally on your own.

CHAPTER 5

I WAS A BLEEDER NOW

I turned away from the SK trailhead's posted warning. I knew that going to the river and back in a day was doable, as long as you were in shape, started out early, took a main trail and stayed on it, carried enough water, and avoided the hottest months of the year—July and August. With my five 16.9-ounce bottled waters, I was carrying just over two quarts—about the same as Margaret Bradley. But I knew my route was a for-sure 17 miles, not actually 28. And the South Kaibab, unlike the Grandview and Tonto trails, would typically have other people on it—although not always as many as today. It was a Saturday in June, a peak day for Grand Canyon SK foot traffic.

I took my daypack off my shoulder, unzipped the little pocket at the top, and quick-checked my cell phone for my start time: 4:45 AM. I'd lost my running watch a few weeks earlier, during a workout high up on the Ridge Trail in Los Angeles. After searching for it in the brush, I didn't bother replacing it. In what was for me a rare moment of Zen-like clarity, I'd decided that perhaps it was the Universe trying to tell me something: There was more to running than checking pace times. I'd relaxed when it came to workouts—just noting the time on the microwave's clock in the kitchen as I headed out the door and when I returned. But today was a special challenge. Time mattered.

I picked up my daypack, slipped my arms through both straps, pulled the bill of my cap down tight, and began to run. I trotted down a half-dozen rough stone steps to a smooth, gray dirt straightaway with a gradual decline: the start of the South Kaibab Trail. There were hikers strung out in front of me as I began my descent, the Canyon barely visible in the semi-darkness. On my right, a shoulder-high retaining wall of sand-colored rocks was positioned tightly in place without mortar. On my left, a row of low guide stones lined the way. There was the feel of a well-maintained, almost manicured trail here; the professional-looking retaining wall, the orderly row of rocks on my left. But I knew things would change drastically—and soon.

A group of young hikers necessitated my first "On your left!" Ahead were more of them—some solo, some in twos and threes, some in groups. I tried to get past them all without slowing down too much, while keeping an eye on the drop at the edge of the trail.

After a few dozen yards, the trail cut left, and the descent grew steeper. As I made the turn, I went around a young male hiking solo, and then a bunch of chatty 20-somethings. The route remained eerily smooth here; another high retaining wall buttressed the rock and dirt above the turn, guide stones continuing along the outside edge.

Then, the trail hung out over a precipice, the guide stones all but disappeared, and there was a barely lit view out over the Canyon. Around a bend was the first of the water breaks that directed rainwater off the trail. This break was made up of two logs, rather than the usual parallel rows of low rocks with a couple feet separating them. I jumped over the logs.

I was running on the gray-white dirt of the Kaibab Limestone that was several hundred feet deep and capped the South Rim. Its chalk-colored formations climbed the Canyon walls around me. The limestone was laid down about 250 million years ago. At the time, the area was covered by the Kaibab Sea extending over most of present-day Arizona and reaching south to Mexico. The sea had west-to-east transgressive cycles, ebbing and flowing over millions of years, in keeping with fluctuating global ocean levels. Many of the marine fossils found in the Canyon, especially at the western end, were complete and without abrasions, indicating calm waters and little movement of their location in that ancient world. The fossils were whispers from so long ago that it staggered the imagination. And my journey through time was only just beginning.

At the next turn, there were some low, twisted cedar trees and pinyon pines on an outcropping. There was also a rustic wooden sign:

"When mules pass
Stand to the side of the trail
Follow mule guides instructions"

There would be no mule trains heading into the Canyon this early in the morning, but further down, I could encounter them making their way up from Phantom Ranch. On my Bright Angel ascent, there could be a tourist horse convoy or two to contend with. In either case, I would need to step aside, wait for them to pass, and lose time.

After the mule train warning, there was a hint of rougher trail to come. Scattered rocky fragments littered the way, and the angle of the descent increased. I zigzagged down a series of serpentine switchbacks stacked vertical against the Canyon wall. Here, the outer edge of the trail was marked in places by more of the rocks that helped guide my way, as I picked off additional hikers. This was a part of the route to make good time, and I increased my speed.

A few turns after the warning sign, I encountered the first of the SK's hundreds of cross-trail logs. Spaced several feet apart, the two-and-a-half-foot logs terraced sections of the trail all the way to the bottom. They held the earth in place against erosion from rain, winter snow, and runoff. I barely needed to raise my feet to go over these first logs. They were half-buried, almost flush with the ground, the trail between each smooth. Further down, they became treacherous, exposed by the elements, sitting high above the dirt, with rough spikes driven through both ends to hold them in place. The spikes protruded up to a quarter inch—enough to catch the toe of a running shoe. I needed to avoid a nasty, danger-ous, even fatal fall.

I was a bleeder now.

The cause was my medication, particularly the blood thinners to lower my blood pressure: aspirin and Plavix. As a result, small cuts bled longer; larger cuts were serious, the bleeding difficult to stem. Even routine shaving nicks, skinned knees, and minor abrasions produced the red stuff in hard-to-stop fashion. I also regularly picked up nasty-looking bruises, sometimes seemingly at the slightest impact. They radiated gruesome, mutating, blue-black-red-yellow discoloration that lasted for days. Accidentally banging an elbow or a knee on something—whether on a run, or simply walking around the house—could create a huge swath of a bruise surrounding the point of contact. I dinged an elbow on a doorframe one day, and the resulting bruise began a couple inches above the elbow, circled all the way around my arm, and travelled down to just a couple of inches above my hand.

"You have internal bleeding!" Kathy said to me with alarm when she saw the huge bruise.

Doctor Stephens had warned me that internal bleeding was dangerous, a blow to the head potentially fatal. This made a fall especially risky on the stretches of the SK filled with the cross-trail logs and their protruding spikes. What if I tripped and hit my head on the hard wood or, worse, landed on one of those spikes? I didn't want to even think about that. Never mind the possibility of fatally flying over the edge in the trickiest places.

I picked off more of the hikers. I wondered how long it would be before I caught the last of them. Sometimes they heard my footsteps and moved over on their own. Sometimes someone said "Runner!" to interrupt the chatter of their fellow hikers. A bunch of kids I took to be Boy Scouts, along with a couple adult supervisors, pulled over single file, halted against the wall of the Canyon.

"Thanks!" I said as I made my way around them.

I'd been a Boy Scout once, when I was 10 years old, only to find myself at odds with the rules and the structure, the quasi-military nature of it: uniforms, earning achievement badges, learning the different types of rope knots (slip, square, two half-hitches, bowline, and the rest). I reluctantly participated in a weekend camping trip and couldn't wait for it to be over. The entire time, I wished I could go off by myself to a lake that was nearby and just enjoy spotting sunbathing turtles. Maybe find some frogs and tadpoles.

My Boy Scout experience reflected my loner status, both self and at times peer-group inflicted. Perhaps that smacked of *The Loneliness of the Long Distance Runner*—the movie from the early 1960s and the short story it was based on. Except I didn't find distance running lonely at all; I found it liberating, exhilarating, and *fun*.

I rounded another sharp switchback, and the cross-trail logs turned treacherous, eroded with uneven dirt between them. As I high-stepped my way down to the next turn, which was tight and narrow without any rocks lining the outer edge, I stayed to my right on the inside. The trail here bore no resemblance to those manicured, first few hundred yards at the start.

As I ran, my daypack—bulky and heavy with its bottled waters—jolted me, banging against my back with each step. I hadn't trained with the daypack full of bottled waters and now thought that perhaps I should have.

Next, the trail became surprisingly even again, until a water break made up of twin, foot-high rectangles of rock crossed in front of me. I jumped both rows and continued running, the section up ahead smooth as it made its way down a medium incline. A sign appeared on my left. It was mounted on twin metal posts and once again featured the outline of the thirsty hiker with its warning. Presumably, it was intended for anyone who had ignored or missed the warning up top.

Here's the thing about doing the Grand Canyon: It's the opposite of hiking—or running—a mountain. On your way up a mountain, fitness, training, and your general physical limitations confront you pretty much immediately. If you run out of gas, you can simply turn around and head back down. You're disappointed—a summit you didn't reach, some target elevation missed, a landmark not achieved—but you know that the easiest part remains: the hike or the run back down.

At the Grand Canyon, you don't start out going up. You start out going *down*. There's no confrontation with your limitations, due to any lack of training, fitness, or even thirst. At least not initially. There's only the deceptive ease of the descent. The "mountain" involved—the ascent back to the rim—doesn't come until the very end.

I saw tourists routinely walking down the easily accessed Bright Angel Trail—located near the Maswick and Bright Angel lodges, and with convenient parking—as if on an afternoon stroll. Sometimes they wore sandals, carrying little to no water, with no idea what they were in for. I'd seen it, coming up Bright Angel on my practice hike. I was dumbfounded to have people breezily descend past me into the Canyon, oblivious to the Herculean task of climbing back out. Things would get tougher for them the further down they went. Sometimes, that was all the way to Indian Garden, four and a half miles of trail and 3,000 feet below the rim, or even past there as the route worked its way down to the Devil's Corkscrew. They treated the Grand Canyon like it was some sort of semi-arid, dirt-and-rock Disneyland Arizona.

Rescues were necessary, even evacuations by helicopters stationed at the airfield just south of the park. Some days, rangers were posted at the first Rest House, a mile and a half down Bright Angel from the rim. Their job was to try to talk the clueless and unprepared out of going any further. Sometimes the people listened; sometimes they ignored the advice.

Around me, the air was still cool, but the temperature was already creeping up into the low 50s. The sky was brightening, the Canyon becoming more visible as I ran up behind a pair of hikers who were slow to move over. The one on the left heard my footsteps and did a sideways stutter-step shuffle as I passed them a little too close to the edge for safety's sake. I'd need to be more careful.

The trail changed to a stretch covered in squared rocks that looked like cobblestones—no doubt placed to combat water erosion and washouts, and to counter the wear of the SK's mule trains with their pounding hoofs and weighted loads. The paving stones disappeared after a dozen yards, and the route became dirt once more.

Without breaking stride, I jumped another water break. There were juniper and pinyon trees along the route here, and good-sized rocks lined both sides of the trail as I caught a glimpse out over the Canyon. I rounded a bend, and the trail changed from the pale dirt of Kaibab Limestone to a reddish brown. I was descending into the Toroweap Formation, composed of gypsum and shale along with sandstone. The rocks represented what was the coastal shoreline of the ancient Kaibab Sea—or, more exactly, a series of seas that came and went over tens of millions of years. As time passed, the sand was compacted by the pressure of subsequent overlying deposits, hardening into rock mixed with minerals.

I had a passing knowledge of geology, courtesy of a college freshman course that was taken as part of fulfilling the science requirement for my liberal arts degree. Also, I was an avid rock collector as a kid: laminated sandstone, banded gneiss, granite, feldspar, quartz, obsidian, and little sheets of mica displayed in sectioned-off squares in my father's emptied Dutch Masters cigar boxes. Fossils were a special category of my rock collection and endlessly fascinating to me.

Once, on a family vacation when we were driving through Italy, we picnicked by the side of the road in the countryside. Wandering around, I spotted an odd sandy-colored chunk of rock with large spirals embedded in it. I picked it up. Was it part of some ancient Roman column ornamentation, I wondered? Only later in a biology class did I realize my odd chunk of rock was an Ammonite fossil. Ammonites created elaborate spiral shells, and based on having nine teeth, it's thought their closest living relative was the octopus. And like an octopus, Ammonites almost certainly propelled themselves by shooting a jet of water and travelling backwards. Some were smaller than my fossil, and some were as big as five feet in diameter.

I was running on a lazy, nearly flat, red-dirt S-curve as the South Kaibab lateralled around the side of the Canyon. The drop to my left was precipitous and without guide stones. There were views of the Tonto Platform off in the distance below. On the SK, small, scattered cedar trees provided sporadic greenery. The grade here was the barest of inclines, with a rising wall of rock on my right that, in all likelihood, had been blasted by dynamite to create the trail.

I passed two women hiking together. The outer one stepped in behind her partner; a guy walked solo just ahead of them. The pass was tight, and I nicked one of the woman's arms, a "Sorry!" hurled over my shoulder. An "On your left" from me got the guy to move over.

The cross-trail logs reappeared, a ladder of the rutted obstacles heading down in front of me. I needed to slow up, the footing tricky. I hadn't done a face plant yet, and I wanted to keep it that way.

The last time I'd gone down was a nasty fall four years ago, and that was nowhere near the Grand Canyon. In fact, it happened in Los Angeles following my return from a 2008 Day at the Beach 5K race victory while on a Kennebunkport, Maine family vacation. I'd won my new 60-69 age group with a 24:20 (24 minutes and 20 seconds) time and a 7:51 pace. I was pleased that it was 28 seconds faster than my time in the race the prior year, which had come just a few months after my emergency angioplasty. And it was more than two minutes faster than my artery-clogged performance seven months before the angioplasty, when I'd struggled across the finish line. The 24:20 was still a long way from the 18:57 I'd done at the 1984 Samurai 5K in Los Angeles—a 6:06 pace—during a short-lived return to running in my 30s. But I was in my 60s now and happy just to break eight minutes a mile.

The confidence I gained from the 5K race victory in Maine had been quickly dispelled back in L.A. two weeks later. I was starting out on my regular three-mile Tuesday morning run, heading up the Laurel Canyon Boulevard sidewalk on my way to Fryman Canyon. In front of me, a group of exercise walkers moved along at their own pace, chatting away among themselves, blocking my way. In order to pass them, I hopped onto the road and ran along the edge of the pavement. After half a dozen yards, I jumped up to return to the sidewalk. The next thing I knew, I was in free fall. My face smashed into the curb.

I picked myself up quickly, my nose bloody, blood on a knee as well. I was stunned. Somehow, I'd missed my footing. I was angry and embarrassed. Not only had my body betrayed me, there were witnesses.

"Are you okay?" It was one of the walkers.

"I'm okay," I lied. I turned and started to walk back to the house, cursing out loud once I was out of their earshot. My knee and my nose were bleeding and throbbing. I started to jog, rounded the corner, and headed back up the familiar incline of our street. After cleaning up in the bathroom—the bleeding difficult to stem with the effects of my blood thinners—I applied a couple Band-Aids and went back outside.

I ran the three-mile course, paying close attention in a way I'd never had to do before: I watched my feet, as well as the route up ahead. I ran faster than usual, perhaps trying to prove something. But I knew that how I ran had been irrevocably changed. It would never be so carefree again. Without extra focus, there could be another disconnect between what I was thinking of as routine physical effort and what my body actually did when attempting to execute it.

That day on Laurel Canyon was the last time I'd fallen. But near misses—barely recovering my balance following a trip or stumble on a trail—were not uncommon. No longer being able to count on sure footing, I'd begun to chant cadence mantras in my head while I ran. It was a way to hone in on my foot mechanics and concentrate: "*Watch your step, plant your foot; watch your step, plant your foot; watch your step, plant your foot.*" Or "*Run, step, plant foot firm; run, step, plant foot firm; run, step, plant foot firm.*"

Late in a long Sunday run, especially on local hilly canyon trails with their uneven surfaces, rocks, tree roots, and general unpredictability, the cadence could devolve into an almost mindless 1-2-3-4-5 foot-strike count: "*Watch your step, bam, bam; watch your step, bam, bam; watch your step, bam, bam.*" My footsteps matched the cadence, a rhythm to it. I paid close attention to how I landed my feet, especially when I was tired and working to hold form, so

     RICK MATER

as to not get sloppy and catch my foot on something or make some other misstep. Sometimes I even chanted out loud.

Today, in the Grand Canyon, I ran with that extra concentration needed for movements that had once come naturally, my senses on high alert as I high-stepped down the cross-trail logs. "*Trot, trot, step; trot, trot, step; trot, trot, step.*"

Things grew quiet, the chatter of the larger groups now behind me. After a stretch of gentle curves and almost level running, the trail descended sharply; a sheer drop of several hundred feet was on my left, a wall of rock on my right.

Abruptly, rows of rock paved the way. They had been fashioned into foot-long rectangles, placed close together, three across and almost even with the ground. The terracing quickly became an uneven jumble, and I needed to watch my step, the stones out of place and appearing as if they had started to slide down into the Canyon. The trail here was in the worst shape I'd encountered so far. I slowed down and took things carefully.

Immediately up ahead, there was a switchback where a pair of large slabs of rock stood at an outcropping. A low wooden sign on a post announced: "OOH AAH POINT." With no one occupying the small area of the outcropping, I paused briefly to go out onto the rocky precipice and take in the unobstructed panoramic vista. For the first time on the route, the Grand Canyon truly opened up before me.

The North Rim was ten miles across the way, as the crow flies. The rising sun, still low on the horizon, illuminated steep escarpments, stark eroded bluffs, deep ravines, and the vast landscape. The early morning light created soft, dusky purples, pinks, and browns, reflecting off the various rock strata, and there were black-shadowed places the sun couldn't yet reach.

Below, front and center, O'Neill Butte rose up like a castle fortress, its rock layers leading up to a narrow flat top, perhaps only 20 or 30 feet across. The butte was aglow, bathed in sunlight. From my vantage point, I could see the ribbon of SK curving its way past it, dropping down to Skeleton Point, then the Tonto Platform and the east-west split of the river gorge with its rugged cliffs where, even further below, and out of sight the Colorado ran through it.

There was tragedy along with beauty at Ooh Aah Point, as recounted in *Death in Grand Canyon*. Early on the morning of October 3, 2001, 13-year-old Hannah Stehlin and her father and brother were on a day hike from the South Rim to the river and back. They stopped to take photos at Ooh Aah Point, and also so Hannah could pet some mules that were there with a work crew. Her father and brother went back onto the trail, heard a noise behind them, turned, and discovered Hannah had vanished. Going over to the edge, they spotted her body, 177 feet below.

Once you've lost a child, it changes everything. You read *When Bad Things Happen to Good People*. You accept the condolences from friends, family, and co-workers. You eventually go on. But your life will never be the same.

CHAPTER 6

WRONG TURN AT CEDAR RIDGE

I stepped back from the Ooh Aah Point precipice and resumed running. Below Ooh Aah Point, the trail intensified as the descent steepened. First, it was paved with rocks cut roughly in the shape and size of bricks to once again strengthen the route against erosion and pounding hoofs. There was a wavy unevenness to the surface, a tight fit between the stones. Other stones marked the Canyon side of the trail and gave notice of the vertical drop.

The paving stones were quickly gone. Soon, some of the toughest of the SK's cross-trail logs came into view. These were gnarled and curved, like the tree trunks and branches they once had been, with clean flat surfaces in places that showed the cut of the saw. There were the thick, protruding spikes, two and sometimes three of them to a log. I lifted my lead foot over each cross-trail log, followed by my trailing foot, taking care to clear it as if I was jumping through a tire drill on an obstacle course.

The trail next dropped into the Coconino Sandstone formation, which had been sand dunes 260 million years ago. Cross-bedding lines were visible in places where winds had swept the now-petrified sand in ever-changing directions. The landscape around me was rocky and barren, except for a few more of the small pinyon pines, along with some sage and mesquite, and cedar trees with their twisted trunks and stunted height.

The so-called cedar trees were actually Utah junipers, but they had become semi-officially "cedars," the upcoming Cedar Ridge named—or misnamed—for them. One story was that early settlers confused the junipers with cedars from back east, and the name stuck. The junipers were amazing trees. They lived for hundreds of years; one in Utah was over a thousand years old. Their secret was an extensive, hidden underground root system used to extract water from a few fractures in the surrounding surface rock as a means of survival in the Canyon's semi-arid climate.

The cedars bore berries that provided sustenance to rabbits, coyotes, and birds. The Canyon's early Native Americans used their seeds for beading necklaces and bracelets. I suspected they were the wood source for the cross-trail logs, but when I asked a ranger at the Visitor Center, he responded, "Nobody's ever asked me that. I have no idea."

Where the trail cut sharply at a switchback, I encountered another step-like series of cross-trail logs. The inside of the trail here was marked with rectangular stones; a ditch on the other side of them provided drainage for the rains when they came. The drainage fed into the water breaks, which sent the rain off into the Canyon below.

The cross-trail logs, the drainage system with its water breaks, the guide stones that lined the way, the brief sections paved with stones—all of it reflected that the South Kaibab Trail was constructed by experienced engineers. Working from December 1924 to June 1925 to build it, one crew started at the South Rim, another at the Colorado River; they blasted their way through solid rock, improving upon the original, more rudimentary Native American route.

The SK dropped 4,700 vertical feet in 6.5 miles and was uniformly designed to be four feet wide. The route cut through eight major geological formations—or more, depending as to how exactly the layers were broken down and counted—on its journey down to the Colorado, where it met the 1.6 to two-billion-year-old Vishnu Schist formation of the inner gorge.

The SK's switchbacks were graded to be less steep than those of the Bright Angel Trail, an 18% maximum versus the sometimes 38% of Bright Angel. More switchbacks per elevation gain on the SK made for a less extreme climb out, compared with Bright Angel's brutal Jacob's Ladder finish.

But there was that issue other than steepness that made coming back up the South Kaibab a questionable, even dangerous proposition. The route was selected because the vast majority of it was constantly in the sun. This resulted in a trail that was more accessible year-round, with snow less likely to remain an obstacle in the spring. However, that same sun exposure caused the trail to be brutally hot in the summer months. It was risky to ascend the SK with all that exposed ridgeline to traverse, and unlike the Bright Angel Trail, no water available on the route.

Guidebooks, park rangers, and a friend of mine in Los Angeles who'd once hiked back up the SK had all warned against trying it. That pal who hiked to the river and back on the South Kaibab told me how he'd started out too late in the morning and didn't arrive at Phantom Ranch until early afternoon, when the gorge was already over 100 degrees. On his way back up the SK, he baked in the sun. Dehydration set in, along with its panic.

"I ran out of water maybe a third of the way back up," he told me. "The sun was relentless. I began to hallucinate. It was September, and I wasn't running into anybody coming down—or going back up, for that matter. By the time I realized what bad shape I was in, it was too late."

"How did you make it out?" I said,

"I finally encountered some hikers coming down who gave me some water. The whole thing was scary as hell. One of the worst experiences of my life."

For me today, I saw more switchbacks with tight turns up ahead, as I cadence-counted my way down. I hugged the inside of the trail for safety, adjusting my running and going slower. Two guys, perhaps in their 30s, were walking up ahead and making good time. I was surprised to see them and hoped they were the last of the hikers. One of them stepped aside, making them single-file, and said, "Have a good one!"

I responded with "Thanks!"

The route wound around the Canyon wall, the view more expansive at each successive turn: the Tonto Platform below, the river gorge with the still invisible Colorado cutting through it, and the North Rim across the way. There were more tight switchbacks and cross-trail logs with deep-ruts in between them. Squat chunks of rock lined the edge, marking the calamitous drop, the trail clearly blasted out of the mass of Supai rock on my right. I hit a stretch so dangerous that I slowed to barely a jog at all. There was a crudeness to the route here, the cross-trail logs covered by dirt that, despite the water breaks, had flowed as mud during the rainy season.

I jumped between the dirt-encrusted logs until I reached a sharp switchback and yet another ladder of cross-trail logs. A water break abruptly interrupted the way with foot-high rocks, and I slowed even more. At a curve, O'Neill Butte appeared in front of me, below and directly ahead.

Emerging from between rock slabs that were on either side of the trail, I came out onto a narrow ridgeline vertical above the Canyon. I was running along Windy Ridge. Regardless of the name, there was only a mild breeze today. The entire width of the trail was perched atop the slender ridgeline, low guide stones lining the way.

I moved at a careful jog, wary of the precipitous drops as I ran the few dozen yards of narrow, exposed trail covered in cobblestone-like chunks of rock and reached Windy Ridge Point. Here, the route angled dramatically out over the Canyon·on a lofty, three-sided perch, and I slowed to take in the views. It was as if Ooh Aah Point with its vistas had been plunked down here lower in the Canyon. Everything around me seemed closer, felt more tangible, almost like I could reach out and touch the Tonto Platform below with its network of eroded ravines and the river gorge snaking through it.

Then, the SK cut right and dived sharply, with more of the crude, cobblestone-like paving. I continued running at a careful pace, the trail rough in the extreme here, the surface uneven and interrupted by stone water breaks with foot-deep drops. Just before I reached a switchback that cut to my left, the cobblestone rocks gave way to dirt.

O'Neill Butte became my beacon as I continued my descent, the water breaks now made of wood here, the route treacherous. Cross-trail logs made another appearance, bunched close together. I kept my pace slow and careful in a high-stepping cadence run, landing in between the logs: "*Trot, trot, step; trot, trot, step; trot, trot, step.*"

At a particularly nasty wood water break created by a pair of high-rising logs, I tripped and stumbled but regained my balance after nearly taking a header.

"Shit!" That was close.

CEDAR RIDGE

The SK became wider and smoother, opening up before me. Some juniper trees populated the area as the route descended into the Hermit Shale Formation, that was left behind by an ancient river system and a swampy environment. Composed of sandstone and siltstone that created much of the red hue that painted parts of the Canyon, the Hermit Shale's color came from iron oxide in the up-to-900-foot-thick formation.

The cross-trail logs disappeared, the trail smooth dirt as I let loose with the freedom of open downhill running. Legs strong, breathing relaxed, I picked up speed heading down towards Cedar Ridge. I was a mile and a half from the SK trailhead and a thousand feet below the South Rim, feeling like the confident old pro. Even the last-minute appearance of some semi-submerged cross-trail logs didn't slow me down much, as I leapt over them, maintaining my momentum.

It was like I was back in Los Angeles on my Sunday morning long run, coming down from Mulholland on the Ridge Trail, increasing my speed as I rounded the curve below the Coldwater Overlook. Dodging the weeping boughs of a lone pepper tree, I reached the stretch where the route leveled off for several dozen yards, and I slowed as I ran along the ridgeline with drops and views of Fryman Canyon off to either side.

Ever since my life should have ended five years ago, I gave a triumphant fist-pump as I arrived at this portion of the Ridge Trail, while I announced out loud, "Look, Ma! I'm on top of the world!" It was a shout out to my mother who died tragically in 1994 at age 70 from a pulmonary embolism. The line was adapted from James Cagney's "Made it, Ma! Top of the world!" as he met his demise in the gangster movie *White Heat*, which I'd seen multiple times on Saturday morning TV as a young kid growing up in New Jersey, before we moved to Munich. The scene had stayed with me.

After a few more strides, I added, "Four stents, 64, and still at it!" It had once been, "Three stents, 63, and still at it!" Before that, it was 62, 61, and 60, dating back to my first spontaneous declaration after escaping the should-have-been-massive fatal heart attack at 59. A celebration of still being alive and kicking—and running.

Today in the Grand Canyon, it felt like that triumphant fist-pump top-of-the-world moment as I came flying down the South Kaibab Trail and arrived at Cedar Ridge's broad expanse of reddish dark dirt interrupted only by low brush, a few cedar trees, and some rocks and boulders strewn about.

Up ahead, I could see a dead-end drop-off fast approaching as the route narrowed into a V leading out onto a slender, rocky outcrop. Something wasn't right. I slowed, came to a stop, and looked around. Confused and disoriented, surrounded by the vastness of the Canyon, I sized up my situation. In front of me was the tapered dead-end. To my left was a steep drop-off. To my right, a large boulder sat next to a bleached, leafless cedar tree lying dead on the ground, its branches angling starkly skyward.

Where the hell was I?

A young guy appeared, trudging up toward me. He seemed barely out of his teens. He wore jeans, a green sweatshirt, a baseball cap, and carried a daypack strapped over his shoulders. Where had he come from? I thought I'd picked off all the hikers.

"Wrong turn?" I said.

"Yeah, guess so," he mumbled, and he hiked up past me.

Damn. At least I wasn't alone in my error. This kid was probably 40 years my junior. But a mistake in your twenties was just a mistake. A mistake at 64 could be because you're losing it—the diminution of your faculties or maybe even the beginning of Alzheimer's confusion.

And Alzheimer's wasn't far-fetched. We'd just had a heart-wrenching case in the family. My late mother's younger brother in England, once gregarious and youthful, had been reduced to a lingering vegetative state. I'd visited him in 2010, housed in a hospital ward with four other old guys after he could no longer be cared for at home, even by my devoted aunt, a retired nurse. She'd told me how helpless she felt as he peed in the hallway instead of the bathroom at their house and became unable to recollect anything of his life, and often incapable of recognizing anyone in his family.

The disease could be genetic, like inheriting my mother's pulmonary problems. I'd already confronted what could be my own precursor-to-Alzheimer's mental confusion on a recent run in L.A. It had me concerned, and I was on the lookout for more symptoms, wondering what I would do if I had to confront the disease head on.

I turned and jogged uphill past the young guy. Then, I took a left to get back on what I judged to be the correct route. Immediately, I saw a rustic wooden sign posted in front of a small, twisted, leafless cedar tree, a circle of large stones at its base.

The sign read: "Cedar Ridge."

So it was all just a silly mistake. I'd drifted too far to the western edge of the ridge, somehow not noticing the sign and bearing sharply left just before it. So much for my practice hike, which had convinced me I knew the route. I would need to pay closer attention the rest of the way. I picked up speed as I headed past the sign. I was glad I had that detailed Canyon trail map in my daypack, along with the flashlight, a power bar, and all those bottled waters.

CHAPTER 7

ALZHEIMER'S?

The hint of possible Alzheimer's I'd recently experienced in Los Angeles was far more alarming than today's Cedar Ridge confusion. In fact, I wondered if it set the stage for my own eventual version of Henry Fonda's panicked, geriatric dash through the woods in the Oscar-winning film *On Golden Pond*—desperate to recognize surroundings that were now foreign to him, despite having visited his beloved pond for years.

I'd been on a routine weekday three-mile run in L.A., making my way uphill on a gentle, winding portion of road. On my right, there were towering plants, 15 feet high, and a wooden fence of upright planks that enclosed an unseen house. On my left was a steep embankment covered in ivy and trees that enshrouded another house. As I ran on the pavement through the tunnel of foliage and hidden houses, I gazed around and realized *I couldn't recognize where I was.*

I knew I was on a run, but where?

I didn't panic.

I kept going at a steady pace, up the curve of the hill. Just keep running, I told myself, as I continued to look around for something familiar. The sun was shining brightly around me, everything quite lovely, as I thought, "*This is so odd.*"

The wall of tall plants ended abruptly, and I arrived at a fork in the road. Instantly, I recognized everything. To my right was Iredell Lane where, a little way further up, I had a one-mile-from-our-house workout marker, a driveway that I'd clocked on my car odometer, and where I'd turned around just short of reaching it on the day of my heart attack. On the left, the steep Iredell Road hill led up to a trailhead that I sometimes used to head up to Mulholland on my Sunday long runs.

I'd run this route literally hundreds of times.

The whole episode lasted maybe ten seconds.

I decided I would need to do some research about Alzheimer's when I got back home. I didn't tell Kathy. She had enough issues already, with the dozen years between us and her perception of me getting older ahead of her . . . and I was.

I Googled Alzheimer's and scrutinized ten early warning signs, including memory loss that disrupts daily life (e.g., forgetting appointments); challenges in planning and solving problems such as paying bills or balancing your checkbook; and trouble completing familiar tasks at work, at home, and in daily life (e.g., driving to a familiar location).

And we had that Alzheimer's history in the family. I'd experienced it firsthand when I'd been with my Uncle Jacques on a visit to England six years earlier. He got us lost driving near his house, heading the wrong way down a one-way street. My aunt was next him in the front, and I was in the back seat.

"Jacques! You're going the wrong way!" said my aunt.

My uncle made an abrupt U-turn and almost hit another vehicle, experiencing what no one knew at the time was early Alzheimer's confusion. Kathy and the girls were with me on that trip, and I was glad that most of the time Jacques was still his old self and Cassidy and Jamie got to know him that way.

On my next trip to England, I was solo. I found myself pushing Jacques in a wheelchair when he could no longer reliably walk from his house to my cousin's nearby. Then came that final visit: Meeting my aunt and her driving us to the hospital ward that my uncle shared with four other guys about his age, which was 78. Anne talking to him as if he understood everything, when it was clear he had only a vague notion of who she was and no idea whatsoever who I was. Jacques, sitting in a chair next to his bed, hunched over while Anne spoon-fed him treats—asparagus and his favorite canned fish—as he chewed, eyes vacant, unrecognizing, lifeless. Anne, talking away to him as if he was still just fine.

"Jacques, you remember Rick, Joan's oldest son? Well, he's here to visit."

My uncle, with just the slightest move of the head my way, sitting, propped up by pillows, giving no response. Anne, looking back and forth between us, as if trying to will him to say something to me.

Another Alzheimer's symptom: confusion with time and place (e.g., forgetting how you got somewhere).

Damn.

That was too close to home, considering what had happened to me in Fryman Canyon. But I was perfectly aware of how I'd gotten there. Well, maybe not. I knew that I was on a workout. But I couldn't have said how I got there, because I didn't know where I was.

I read another symptom: struggling with words in conversation.

Damn, again.

I'd been playing the Conversation Game for several years now, ever since I started to have problems recalling the name of a rock band, movie, book, actor, or a TV show while talking with someone. I began to think a step ahead in conversations, especially at the office, learning to do last-minute verbal gymnastics as I got to a proper name or piece of information that was going to come up in a sentence or two or three and realized I was drawing a blank. I'd dance around using the specific word or name. I wanted to avoid putting myself in the embarrassing position of having to acknowledge I couldn't come up with it. I was loath to bemoan getting older with some comment about having a "brain fart" or, God forbid, "a senior moment."

But the online research information also indicated that trouble finding the right word was typical of aging—not just of Alzheimer's. In fact, each of the various symptoms was noted on the website as "typical age-related change," which also included misplacing things, trouble retracing your steps, poor judgment, and withdrawal from work or social obligations. So, when symptoms first showed up, it was difficult to know what was a function of getting older and what was the beginning signs of Alzheimer's. Until and unless the symptoms became worse over time—minor became major, sometimes became often—you just couldn't know for sure.

Alarmingly, I'd also started to notice occasional misuses of words or spelling mistakes cropping up in my emails at work. It could be as simple as the wrong use of "it's" versus "its." More troubling was "seen" instead of "scene," "should" instead of "showed," and "addition" instead of "edition." I'd begun to be certain to re-read my emails before sending them—ideally, out loud to be sure to catch miscues. Personal emails soon joined the proofreading exercise.

Checking still another website, there was "forgetting recently learned information" as a symptom. This caught my eye, along with what it said could be changes in mood and personality—such as becoming easily upset. Hmmm. There were my annoyed reactions and prickly responses to small things: becoming easily frustrated at misbehaving technology or struggling to figure out something new on my laptop or my BlackBerry. At work, I generally kept my cool. I could rely on a call to IT for a quick, helpful visit when it came to anything involving my computer. Besides, this wasn't something new. Impatience and too-easy frustration were tendencies that always afflicted me. But it was yet one more example of what's normal when you're in your 20s but feels like it could be symptomatic of a problem in your 60s.

A couple websites said there was evidence that running seemed to, at least anecdotally, counter some effects of aging—from combatting deterioration of muscles to aiding better mental health and brain function. But the verdict was out as regards definitive empirical evidence of a positive impact of running on the disease.

After reviewing all the various websites, I made a note to watch for other signs. I knew I would need to pay close attention to symptoms from this moment forward to stay vigilant for Alzheimer's slow slide into oblivion, should I turn out to have the disease. I wanted to be in control of my life before there was change beyond the point of no return.

What would I do if it became clear that I had Alzheimer's and the disease was taking over my brain like it had with my Uncle Jacques? What were my options to not end up like he had—in a hospital or assisted-living facility, half out of my wits, heading to completely out of my wits, in some pathetic state of non-existence?

Should I commit suicide during my fast-closing window of lucidity? That was the logical conclusion. What other choice was there, really?

I didn't want to become my uncle.

CHAPTER 8

THE SAGA OF BUCKEY O'NEILL

After spotting the Cedar Ridge sign, I continued running past a long metal horse-and-mule hitching post to my left that I remembered from my hike. To my right was the trek up to a rustic wooden structure with pit toilets—essentially an outhouse with no running water. Further up ahead, the South Kaibab Trail curved off Cedar Ridge, marked by twin rows of low rocks on either side of the route, but otherwise not terribly easy to make out.

As I followed the SK down off Cedar Ridge, I encountered rocks inlaid like paving stones for a short stretch. They quickly gave way to a ladder of cross-trail logs arranged in a steep descent. Here, the trail's downhill side with its drop was again dangerous. I trotted carefully, lifting my knees, planting my feet, eyes on the trail: "*Trot, trot, step; trot, trot, step; trot, trot, step.*"

From Cedar Ridge to O'Neill Butte, the SK passed through the 1,000-foot-thick Supai Group. Like the Toroweap Formation, Hermit Shale, and Kaibab Limestone above, the rocks around me reflected periods when warm, shallow seas covered the area; the sediments here were laid down 270 million to 320 million years ago. The color of the Supai Group sandstone and limestone varied

The Sk near O'Neille Butte

from rust-shaded to tan, the formation eroding into huge blocks that sometimes broke off and tumbled into the Canyon.

As I headed down a long stretch of rutted cross-trail logs, O'Neill Butte lay ahead. Sharp switchbacks sent me first east, then west, and finally north on my way to the landmark. I passed a couple leafless cedars with their bleached boughs and reached O'Neill Butte, running along beside its base. The top of the butte was up above me; the rest of it fell away below, looking like it was the prow of a colossal ship jutting out over the Tonto.

The trail here was smooth red dirt lined with a row of rocks on either side as I descended along the butte's eastern flank. Things quickly turned challenging. Sizeable water breaks interrupted the route every dozen or so yards. The first one—a row of upright rocks a foot high—suddenly appeared in front of me, followed in a couple feet by another row of rocks in parallel formation, necessitating the usual two jumps. After that, wooden log water breaks alternated with the stone breaks.

I picked up speed as the trail went into a long descent, the path again relatively smooth. To my right was a sloping down hillside covered in boulders that had broken off from the Supai Group. To my left, a hillside full of the boulders led up the butte itself.

BUCKEY O'NEILL

The idea of leaving a legacy behind was on my mind a lot lately, exacerbated by my cardiac issues. It would be interesting to have asked William Owen "Buckey" O'Neill about that. The butte I was running alongside was named in his honor. I wondered what he would have thought. Bemused? Ambivalent? Proud? Would he have come up with an apropos line from one of the poets that he liked to quote, much to his Rough Riders commander Teddy

Roosevelt's delight: Robert Browning, Percy Shelley, or Walt Whitman? Whitman once wrote, "Nothing can happen more beautiful than death." Did O'Neill ever quote that one?

Buckey O'Neill accomplished a lot in a life cut short: frontier sheriff, judge, newspaperman, miner, gambler, adventurer, politician, soldier, and Grand Canyon entrepreneur. In 1879, at age 19, he arrived alone to the Arizona Territory. The region was in its Wild West silver-mining boomtown heyday, an influx of fortune seekers coming from around the country. Eager to try his luck, O'Neill headed first to Tombstone, where Wyatt Earp was the local law enforcement.

Located 30 miles north of the Mexican border in the southern Arizona desert, Tombstone was a notorious mining camp. O'Neill worked as a reporter on the local newspaper, *The Tombstone Epitaph*, which was located across the street from the O.K. Corral. O'Neill became a saloon habitué and gambler, along with such local notables as William "Bat" Masterson, John "Doc" Holliday, and gunslinger Johnny Ringo. It isn't known if O'Neill was in town for the famed O.K. Corral shootout between the Earp Brothers and the Clanton Gang—a battle that was the stuff of legend.

Popular, gregarious, and known for his wit and storytelling, O'Neill hung out in the town's saloons. He invariably had a hand-rolled cigarette, filled with Bull Durham tobacco, dangling from his lips. At almost six feet tall, he was good looking and cut a dashing figure.

After his time in Tombstone, O'Neill settled in Prescott, just south of the Canyon, his home for the next 16 years. He married local 21-year-old teacher and suffragette Pauline Schindler. They had a son, Buckey, Jr., who tragically died just two weeks after being born prematurely. I noted the loss of the child and wondered how he had dealt with it. The young couple adopted another son later the same year.

In 1888, O'Neill was elected sheriff of Yavapai County, which included Prescott. A photo of the mustached O'Neill shows him posed with a hand on the top of the barrel of an upright rifle, a six-shooter and bullet belt around his hips, a sheriff's star pinned on his vest, as he stared into the camera from under a flat-brimmed hat. While sheriff, he led a posse in pursuit of three train robbers. The posse covered 600 miles of Arizona and Utah. During the chase's climactic gunfight, O'Neill's horse was shot out from under him. Despite the setback, the outlaws were captured.

Having made a small fortune investing in an onyx mine that excavated the semi-precious ornamental stone, O'Neill decided not to run for sheriff again and instead focused his efforts on mining in the Grand Canyon. In 1890, he built a cabin on the South Rim, just east of the Bright Angel trailhead, near where the Kolb Brothers would construct their photography studio a dozen years later. During this period, O'Neill split his time between the Canyon and his family in Prescott.

As an aspiring entrepreneur, O'Neill became a partner in copper mining as part of the Grand Canyon Mining Company. But with no railroad to the Canyon, the cost of shipping the ore was prohibitively expensive. So, O'Neill helped build a railroad that would finish laying tracks in 1901. The spur would then be bought out by the Santa Fe Railroad, which brought in tourists when roads and the automobile were sometimes unreliable travel propositions.

On February 15, 1898, in the Havana, Cuba harbor, an explosion sank the visiting warship the USS Maine, killing 260 of its 400 crewmen. The Spanish-American War was on. Assistant Secretary of the Navy Teddy Roosevelt set about using his military connections to get permission to recruit an army unit of irregulars, composed heavily of cowboys from the West—among them O'Neill. Officially known as the First Volunteer Cavalry Regiment, the unit would become legendary as the Rough Riders. Roosevelt was given the rank of Lieutenant Colonel. O'Neill was appointed a captain.

Roosevelt had a romantic notion of war. O'Neill shared his reverence for heroism in battle. He was a favorite of Roosevelt who admired his experience as a sheriff. By all accounts, O'Neill was one of the most popular officers in the Rough Riders.

On July 1, 1898, the Rough Riders came under heavy Spanish fire as part of the prelude to the Battle of San Juan Hill. Captain O'Neill was reported to have openly walked among his men, not taking cover, smoking a cigarette, leading fearlessly by example, despite the risk as Spanish sharpshooters fired on them from tall trees.

When his men expressed concern, O'Neill is reported to have said, "The Spanish bullet isn't made that will kill me." A few minutes later came a rifle crack, and O'Neill went down. A Spanish bullet had struck him in the mouth and traveled out the back of his head. Other soldiers pulled him to safety, but he died within seconds. He was just 38 years old.

A notable statue of O'Neill stands in Prescott, outside of the Yavapai courthouse. The statue commemorates O'Neill's Rough Rider days, depicting him in heroic boots-in-stirrups fashion upon a rearing steed. Solon Borglum, who cast the statue, was the younger brother of artist and sculptor Gutzon Borglum who sculpted Mount Rushmore. When the statue was unveiled in July 1907, a crowd of 7,000 was present in the courthouse square as a band played "America the Beautiful" and former Rough Riders rode in tribute.

Time marches on, and the memory of Buckey O'Neil faded. The construction of the South Kaibab Trail plucked him from obscurity, thanks to the butte that bears his name. Each week, hundreds, even thousands of people pass by the formation in the late spring, summer, and early fall hiking months. Those with Canyon maps and a familiarity with the landmarks know its name. Virtually nobody else does. There's no wooden sign on a post to identify O'Neill Butte, unlike other landmarks: Ooh Aah Point, Cedar Ridge, Skeleton Point. There's no explanatory historical marker bearing a neat little biography to recount O'Neill's life and attach a man to the name. The butte is simply a random, if striking, landmark.

O'Neill wasn't the only one with an affinity for the Canyon; his friend Theodore Roosevelt had it too. President Roosevelt became a visitor and advocate for the Grand Canyon, naming it a National Monument on January 11, 1908. Subsequently, in 1919, Congress declared it a national park.

One wonders if O'Neill's conversations with Roosevelt piqued the latter's curiosity and helped formulate his decision to first visit the Canyon in 1903. Roosevelt and his party descended the Bright Angel Trail, passing O'Neill's cabin on the way. One imagines Roosevelt saw the little house that had served as a home for his esteemed officer. Perhaps he said something to those accompanying him about the brave young captain who quoted poets and died in battle, which to Roosevelt was the epitome of service, duty, and manhood.

Buckey O'Neill's cabin became a part of the Bright Angel Lodge in 1935 during a remodeling of the facility that is one of the main hotels on the South Rim. Today, the cabin is marked with O'Neill's name and is rentable by request. It faces out over the South Rim with wonderful views.

Did Buckey O'Neill make a difference? Certainly, he made an impression on Theodore Roosevelt and others of his time. O'Neill has achieved immortality of a sort. After the rest of us are long gone, O'Neill Butte will still be O'Neill Butte.

Tick, tick, tick.

The trail was relatively smooth as I moved further down the eastern flank of O'Neill Butte. I picked up speed and ran almost as fast as I did during my final descent to Cedar Ridge. As usual, the smooth section didn't last. At a switchback came exposed cross-trail logs. The switchback after that one was tighter, a sharp cutback with a foot-high rock water break necessitating a higher than usual set of jumps. Large Supai blocks clustered ominously up above me. A rocky slope was on my right as the descent wound its way alongside the last of the butte and transitioned to smooth dirt. I picked up speed again.

Out of nowhere, the cross-trail logs returned with a vengeance, forcing me to slow down. The trail here was jarringly uneven, full of seemingly random step-downs, bits and pieces of rock, the cross-trail logs, and the water breaks. Ahead and below, I could see a long, mostly smooth stretch of wide-open ridgeline beckoning.

CHAPTER 9

PANGAEA: THE LAST SUPERCONTINENT

Two hundred and seventy million years ago, the Earth didn't have seven continents. There was only one supercontinent: Pangaea, containing all the planet's land locked together in one immense mass, surrounded by a single, vast ocean: Panthalassa.

As I came down along the base of O'Neill Butte, I was running on what had once been Pangaea—whether as sand dunes, muddy estuaries, or sediment under ancient seas. From the South Rim, down through the Kaibab Limestone, Toroweap Formation, Coconino Sandstone, Hermit Shale, and finally the Supai Group, all of it had originated on Pangaea. Arizona and the rest of North America comprised the northwest portion of the supercontinent and were once located approximately where Greenland is today.

About 300 million years ago, at the start of the Triassic Period, the two huge continents of Gondwana and Laurasia had collided to form Pangaea. Gondwana, in the Southern Hemisphere, was comprised of South America, Africa, India, and Australia. Laurasia was in the Northern Hemisphere and made up of North

America, Greenland, Europe, and most of Asia. Pangaea straddled the equator, the upper third in the Northern Hemisphere and the lower two thirds extending into the Southern Hemisphere.

Pangaea had a diverse climate, from wet and humid coastline to desert interior. Thanks to Pangaea's inland seas and plentiful vegetation, some of Earth's earliest animals flourished near the lush equator and along the coastline. There were the first amphibians, plus turtles, crocodiles, and snakes, as well as grasshoppers, spiders, scorpions, and centipedes. Reef-building corals originated along the shores. The earliest dinosaurs emerged on the supercontinent.

The first true mammals also appeared on Pangaea, living in the woodlands of what would eventually become Europe, which was located along Pangaea's upper eastern coastline. They survived by eating insects and lizards and hunted at night, their tiny stature typical of the earliest mammals. Dinosaurs were the dominant species, and mammals occupied their niche by being small, able to scurry up trees, and otherwise avoiding predators.

Reptiles were one of the few animal groups that pre-dated Pangaea. But the entirety of the Triassic Period—the Age of Reptiles—took place on Pangaea from 252 to 201 million years ago. The first half of the subsequent Jurassic Period also took place on Pangaea as well, ushering in the Age of Dinosaurs.

It was German meteorologist and geophysicist Alfred Wegener who, in a series of 1912 lectures and scientific papers, posited that there had once been such a thing as a supercontinent. He was the one who named it Pangaea ("Pan" from ancient Greek for "entire" or "whole" and "Gaea" for "Mother Earth" or "land"). Wegener proposed that the once-conjoined continents had separated over a long period of geological time by means of what he dubbed "continental drift." He was greeted with skepticism and outright ridicule from the world's scientific community. At the time, most scientists believed in static geology—that things had always essentially been as they were now. The biggest problem with Wagener's theory was his inability to explain a mechanism that caused the continents to move around on the Earth's surface.

Key evidence of the existence of Pangaea came from the fossil record, with species discovered in South America that were the same as some unearthed in Africa, and warm-weather fossils were found in Antarctica. The same extinct plant fossils were found on widely disparate continents. Coal deposits from Poland and North America also matched up in composition. It became clear that certain mountain chains—the Appalachians in the U.S., the Atlas Mountains of North Africa, and the Caledonides of Ireland, England, Greenland, and Scandinavia—were all once part of a single chain, the Central Pangaea Mountains formed by the collision of Gondwana and Laurasia.

When I took geology in college, the concept of plate tectonics was still new. Regarding opposition to Wegener's theory of continental drift, the science only definitively had begun to change in the early 1950s, when, for example, soil samples from India showed that it had once been in the Southern Hemisphere, just as Wegener had predicted. Continental drift got another look, which led to the concept of plate tectonics—the missing mechanism that drove continental movement. It wasn't drift at all, rather a conveyer belt of continents riding on moving tectonic plates.

Wagener didn't live to see the acceptance of his pioneering work. He died at age 50 on an expedition to Greenland in 1930. Along with two other scientists, he starved to death in a blizzard while doing climate research. But Wagener made a difference before he died. He expanded our empirical knowledge of the world around us and how it works. A scientist who thought outside the box, he stood his ground against the forces arrayed against him. Studying climate was his area of expertise, and the fact that he wasn't a geologist had set him up for ridicule. Perhaps his unorthodox background made him uniquely equipped for the task at hand. Being bold and willing to approach geological questions from a different, more original point of view, Wagener initiated a leap in our understanding of the Earth and left a lasting legacy.

Pangaea, fully formed with all the continents conjoined, existed for about 100 million years. Approximately 175 million years ago, like some primordial Atlantis, Pangaea ruptured along its east-west axis between North America and Africa. But, unlike Atlantis, Pangaea didn't sink. North America and Eurasia headed northward, and eventually separated in easterly and westerly directions. South America and Africa split and moved west and east, respectively. Antarctica and Australia, still joined, traveled toward the South Pole. India began a journey eastward, and much later, beginning 35 million years ago, crashed into Asia and produced the Himalayas. It's a collision that continues to this day, with ongoing uplift as the tallest mountains in the world rise even higher.

Over millions of years of incremental tectonic plate shifting, Pangaea's fragmentation eventually resulted in the continents located in the positions we know today.

Treading on Pangaea—exposed by erosion as I descended through geological time—was one of the wonders of the Grand Canyon. Since Pangaea witnessed the origin of most land animals on the planet, including mammals, the supercontinent could, in a sense, be seen as man's ancestral home.

As I plunged down into the past, Canyon vistas representing hundreds of millions of years of geological history opened up before me. These were entirely different worlds from today's temporary version of the planet. The finite and the infinite were in play. With the Grand Canyon and the echoes of the past all around me, my petty preoccupations—and even my not-so-petty ones—and

day-to-day distractions were momentarily transcended. I was in-
terconnected with this world and its changing identities in a new
and different way. Continents moved and recomposed, making all
of us part of a continuum that spanned eons. Our few seconds on
Earth were to be treasured.

Pangaea was visible in plain sight, if you knew to look for it.

CHAPTER 10

SKELETON POINT

Dawn was breaking for real, everything illuminating around me. The trail changed hue, from red to sand-colored, as I ran through the last of the Supai Group. I descended more ladder-like sections of cross-trail logs, which eventually gave way to a modest downward slope that stretched out before me. Below O'Neill Butte, the route turned flat and open without water breaks or cross-trail logs, the ridgeline wide here. The SK went through the middle of it in a straight line marked by low guide stones, so I picked up speed.

I was heading toward a hump-like mini-butte that was maybe a half-mile away. Upon reaching it, I saw that it had a pinnacle of upright rocks along its crest that reminded me of the blades on the back of a Stegosaurus. That dinosaur lived in the late Jurassic Period, 160 million years ago, as the continents of Pangaea travelled to their new destinations and took their life with them—including the dinosaurs.

Past the mini-butte, the ridge broadened further, and I coasted onto a compact, flat, sandy promontory; the surface changed color to a lighter shade of brown. There wasn't another soul in sight. A wooden sign, mounted on a post protruding from a pile of rocks, announced: "SKELETON POINT."

I paused to retrieve one of the bottled waters from my daypack to carry it with me, and I took a sip. Around me was an expanse of dirt and rock that was smaller and more barren than Cedar Ridge. The Tonto Platform was visible 1,000 feet below, carpeted with faded green blackbrush scrub, the Colorado still hidden from view by the walls of the river gorge.

Looking to the East, I could glimpse the course of Margaret Bradley's fatal run. The Tonto Trail was a narrow, hard-to-make-out band of dirt paralleling where the bottom of the South Rim met the platform's expanse. I could see Pattie Butte, named for early prospector and trapper Sylvester Pattie who was credited as the first "American" to visit the Canyon. A bit further was Lonetree Canyon, home to Native American ruins that consisted of stone dwellings at the base of a Tapeats cliff. Somewhere out of sight and further still was Cremation Creek, unlikely to still be flowing this time of year—just like when Bradley's life ended that sweltering July day, with her trapped on the lip of a 130-foot dry waterfall.

I took another swig from the bottled water, twisted the cap back on, and resumed my run. On my left, I passed another of the long metal horse-and-mule hitching posts. Then, the trail dropped to the right off Skeleton Point, like it had at Cedar Ridge, and I followed it down at a good clip.

I was sweating some now, most noticeably around the edge of my Phidippides cap despite its air-holed ventilation. The sun was shining more brightly, everything here being exposed directly to its rays with no shade. I guessed it to still be only 60-something degrees, but the mild temperature was countered by my exertion.

The just-in-case sunglasses were in my daypack if I needed them to combat the brightness. I hadn't worn them in years when running—not since I occasionally used a wraparound pair during my marathon training days. I preferred to take in things around me more naturally, especially here in the Canyon. Sunglasses undermined that pure experience. Just like I never ran while listening to music. In addition, headphones blocked ambient sound, a potential danger when working out on streets in Los Angeles if I was unable to hear an oncoming car or truck.

Besides, I desired to engage the world while running, not shut it out. Running was a time for me to be at one with nature. Well, to be alone with my thoughts—my constant interior monologue, its endless brain chatter—along with nature. On a good day, I could get something accomplished while I ran, as a result of all that mental yammering. Solve a problem by working through it, whether it involved the job, the girls, or . . . *life.*

Sometimes a pop tune with an infectious hook could get stuck in my head—despite no headset music—and interrupt the problem-solving. Or some profound thoughts about existence and its riddles might do it. Or even just my increasing tendency as I got older to review my past life and question decisions, actions, paths taken and not taken. Any number of things could speed though my mind in an ongoing stream of consciousness as I ran.

It was different back when I had running partners for marathon training, and we ran long miles out and back on semi-rustic Mulholland Drive, high above the San Fernando Valley and its suburban sprawl. Or as we ran 20 miles down flat, store-lined Ventura Boulevard below. A group of three or four or five of us, talking about our jobs, the stock market, our kids, as we ran shoulder-to-shoulder, or else as pairs in tandem, one behind the other.

But that was ten and fifteen years ago. Now that I preferred to run solo, I didn't have the distraction of human company. My only company was my runaway brain with its frenetic energy and boundless machinations. Sometimes, it distracted me from truly paying attention to my surroundings on my Sunday long runs—from being at one with nature, or just *being*. Still. Calm. Relaxed. *Living in the moment.* Sometimes I wished I was into Yoga, meditation, or some sort of calming breathing exercise. But that just wasn't me.

At some point recently, the idea of simply relaxing had become anathema. For example, lounging at the beach, a favorite activity of many in Southern California. There was increasingly a feeling to it that I was wasting time—the time I had left. My emergency angioplasty had compounded this, speeding up a process that was already under way. Just hanging around on a weekend off left me with the nagging thought that I should be accomplishing something more.

For me, relaxing on a beach was becoming a lost art. I used to do lots of it. During our honeymoon in Cannes in 1993, I gazed around as I stretched out on the sand. Kathy, in the spirit of the French, was topless, fit and sexy beside me, the both of us twenty years younger. Hanging out by the ocean was a fine activity back then. And there were earlier days spent with friends on the beaches at Venice, Santa Monica, and Malibu, when I first moved to Los Angeles from Berkeley in 1977. Or trips to Zuma Beach with the girls when they were younger. Seemingly endless weekends spent at the beach, *when time was still something I had plenty of.*

Now, my time was compressing up against a finite end point. I thought about what I still wanted to achieve. One major ambition was to follow through on my writing. I had written on and off for years. Some local magazine pieces were published in S.F. and L.A.; one was sold to a glossy national monthly. There were also unpublished essays, fiction, even a one-act play, amounting to many hundreds of pages.

I sometimes thought about my writing during Sunday morning long runs in Los Angeles. Writing was the sort of self-absorbed and inward-looking activity that, for better or worse, felt natural to me. I loved the escape and creativity of it and the feeling that I was accomplishing something that mattered. As well as being a creative outlet, writing was an attempt to come to terms with my life and resolve its many contradictions.

BEAT

Among my literary endeavors, it was my novel *Beat* that mattered the most to me. Finishing *Beat* before my time on the planet was over would allow me to realize something of value in my own hierarchy of what was important. An achievement I could be proud of.

Beat was a *roman à clef* about a time and a place and a group of 20-somethings who passed through it. Young people facing life at a crossroads in San Francisco circa 1976, confronting their vanished 1960s counterculture idealism, and needing to find new paths forward. Its quasi-autobiographical account served to impose structure on my own life and give it importance, value, and worth, while providing order, logic, and *meaning*—with an overlay of fiction—to a time that was all too often filled with chaos, confusion, and pain.

And drug abuse. Lots of drug abuse.

In my next agent go-round, I was tempted to pitch it as an account of a new Lost Generation—San Francisco, our Paris; Vietnam, our crucible rather than the First World War; pot, Quaaludes, and cocaine our libations in place of wine, aperitifs, and F. Scott Fitzgerald's cocktails. But that seemed to be inviting dangerous, lofty comparisons.

A return to rewriting the novel had been at the top of my bucket list, post-angioplasty. I'd put it aside for a few years after agents first considered it, some offering positive comments but no representation.

And *Beat* had a connection to the Grand Canyon. My very first visit had been three years before the timeframe of the novel. I'd travelled to the Canyon with my girlfriend, Honey—who haunted the manuscript's pages like a ghost—on our fateful, final cross-country trip together in my used 1964 VW bus.

The bus was outfitted for the road. I'd constructed a sleeping platform out of two-by-fours and plywood, a mattress resting on top. There was also an ice-powered fridge, curtains strung to cover the windows, and a litter box for our cat. Stickers like "Lick Dick in '72" and "Honk if You're Jesus" adorned the rear bumper. At the Canyon, we'd taken snapshots from the rim, hiked part way down the Bright Angel Trail, and camped in the Kaibab National Forest just outside the park.

The year before our Canyon visit, Honey and I had made the cross-country trip in the opposite direction, heading to California. We were full of youthful optimism and in love, even if nearly broke and subsisting on ten pounds of granola I'd made from the recipe in ex-Merry Prankster Stewart Brand's *Whole Earth Catalogue*. Brand's prodigious book also serialized Gurney Norman's counterculture novel *Divine Right's Trip*, the story of one guy's journey home, "back to the land," in *his* VW bus named "Urge." In my own novel, I'd named the (anti-) hero's VW bus "Kozmic."

I needed to get back to that re-write of *Beat* after today's Canyon run. The task of getting the novel completed and published had assumed epic proportions in my personal universe.

Tick, tick, tick.

CHAPTER 11

WHOA POINT!

was running alone, just the way I liked it. It was as if I had the Grand Canyon to myself as I worked my way down to the switchbacks below Skeleton Point. I got my first view of the Colorado, visible between a break in the gorge wall, the river flowing green and split lengthwise by a sand bar.

Next, I rounded a rock face and was astonished like I'd been my first time here a month ago on my practice hike. The trail went along a ledge, and suddenly it felt as if I was suspended in space out over the Canyon. There was no line of guide stones marking the outside edge and warning of the dangerous drop. It was just me and the narrow trail paralleling the rock face, with a fatal fall if I made a mistake. I slowed my pace for safety and to take in the view. There was the Tonto Platform below, closer now. Beyond it were the rock walls of the inner gorge and more of the green swath of the Colorado.

There was no sign here, no name that I knew for this place. There was nothing on my Grand Canyon map. Just an anonymous beauty of a spot that I'd taken to calling Whoa Point! ever since I stopped and appreciated it a month ago. I couldn't see anyone behind me nor anyone ahead and around the curve of the rock.

A pervasive silence graced the Canyon, broken only by the wind, as the river flowed in the distance. A condor circled high up above to the west; there was no mistaking the huge wings.

I had started the practice hike with my older cousin James, who was down from Oregon and made a twice-a-year Canyon pilgrimage with a group of friends. James was something of an expert on the Grand Canyon and its various trails. Our group took a leisurely walking pace down to Cedar Ridge, with pauses and stops along the way. I'd been impatient to get on with the hike rather than take a break with them, and the idea of doing the Canyon alone appealed to me.

"I'll see you guys at Phantom Ranch," I said to my cousin.

"Are you sure?" he replied, sounding surprised.

"Yeah, I'm feeling like going a bit faster."

I continued on solo, trying out running in a few places. After waiting for them briefly at Phantom Ranch, I decided to finish without them.

On my run today, after a dozen yards of hugging the Whoa Point! rock wall at a slow jog, I picked up the pace. The going was rough as I encountered switchbacks and cross-trail logs along the base of the Redwall Formation looming over the Tonto. Named for its distinctive rust coloring and dating back to 335 million years ago, the Redwall deposit was about 500 feet thick. The color was caused by red sandstone leaching from the Supai and Hermit shale strata above and staining the rock. Behind the red facade, the rock was actually light brown. There were numerous marine fossils in the Redwall, including trilobites, mementos of an equatorial tropical sea that once covered this area. The formation had been a part of the huge continent of Laurentia, moving incrementally but relentlessly across the Earth's crust to eventually collide with Gondwana and form Pangaea.

A metal sign on my right had none of the rustic charm of the wood-lettered signs that signaled landmarks. Perhaps it was directed at workers in the Canyon rather than tourists. It was business-like, small, and easy to miss:

"Kaibab Trail
SOUTH RIM 3.5
PHANTOM RANCH 3.8
Elevation 4,700"

I was almost halfway to Phantom Ranch. At 3,000 feet below the South Rim, I was feeling good, paying attention to my footwork, juggling the uneven weight distribution of the daypack, and carrying the partially emptied water bottle in a hand.

No mule trains were visible ahead; the hikers I'd been passing had been left behind long ago. There was no one that I could see coming up the trail after they'd broke camp at Phantom Ranch. They rarely came up the SK anyway, virtually all of them choosing Bright Angel because of its water spigots at Indian Garden and the Three Mile and the Mile and a Half Rest Houses. Not to mention periodic shade, rather than the South Kaibab's relentless, waterless sun-exposed ridgeline—the site of my pal's dehydrated, potentially fatal climb.

I'd had my own life-threatening experience when it could have all ended for me on that day, four and a half years ago in Fryman Canyon.

CHAPTER 12

HEART ATTACK

FEBRUARY 1, 2007

I headed out the front door for my Thursday morning workout. My running had been in the toilet for weeks. At first, I chalked up the sluggish runs to one of my periodic crash-and-burns. It was tough to train year-round and stay in top form, especially as I got older. Sometimes my body rebelled; my desire and my performance went south. Usually, after a few weeks of motivation gone missing, slower than usual times, and having to drag myself out the door, the problem passed as quickly as it had appeared. A new training cycle began, with motivation reborn and ever better results.

This time, I wasn't pulling out of it. In fact, it was getting worse. Things were happening that had never happened before. I hadn't done a decent Sunday long run in a month. On the last attempt, I needed to cut it down to only 30 minutes—walking most of it. I skipped doing a few of my weekday runs.

The effects of aging? Perhaps. But the decline seemed too far, too fast. I wanted to get some answers.

As I trotted down the front steps, Kathy, Cassidy, and Jamie were in the driveway loading their backpacks into the trunk of Kathy's Corolla.

"Have a great day at school," I said to the girls.

"Bye, Dad," they responded in unison.

"See you later, babe," I told Kathy.

"Bye, Hon," Kathy called back to me as I turned and ran down the slope of our street. At age 59, I'd settled into a like-clockwork routine: a three-mile run every Tuesday and Thursday morning before going into the office, and a six, eight, or ten-miler on Sundays. It was enough training to still permit me to race periodically and be competitive in my age group.

A few hundred yards from the house, I turned right onto Laurel Canyon Boulevard. Moving along the sidewalk, I would soon reach the sanctuary of Fryman Canyon with its quiet residential streets, expensive homes, and the various trailheads leading up into nature-preserved hills populated by rabbits, mule deer, and coyotes.

Slipping between the row of slender conifers that signaled the change from concrete sidewalk to dirt path, I continued for a couple dozen yards and made the turn into Fryman Canyon. I checked my running watch: four minutes. Good. That was already longer than the previous workout when, after only two minutes, I'd felt like I should stop running and walked instead.

Suddenly, I was overwhelmed by the sensation that my body had completely lost the ability to run. I had the thought that, if I really put my mind to it, I could possibly manage another few yards, but that felt foolish—even dangerous. I eased to a stop, like a car that had run out of gas. My hand went to my chest and rubbed at a vague discomfort inside my rib cage.

Immediately, I knew it was my heart.

Jesus. My mind reeled. This couldn't be happening. I prided myself on my health. I rarely spent a day out of the office, sick.

I recovered quickly from the occasional running injury, barely side-lined even for a few days. I'd never had a broken bone, never been hospitalized, never required surgery. Sure, there was the medication, begun five years earlier, that got my rising blood pressure numbers down and lulled me into thinking that things were okay.

I began to walk my workout route. I wasn't in pain. I was in shock, moving forward on some kind of autopilot as I tried to process what was going on. The thought of turning around didn't enter my mind. Several runners passed me. A smattering of exercise walkers and people with their dogs ambled along the side of the road. They smiled and talked among themselves. For them, this was just another day. I was in an alternate universe, where a life could be turned upside down in an instant and where mortality lurked—not off in the distance, but staring me right in the face.

Perhaps I was overreacting. Maybe it wasn't my heart. After all, there was no heaviness in my chest, no tingling in my arms or the left side of my torso, no breathlessness, no feeling faint. Just some clamminess—a coolness to my body, accompanying the vague sensation that something wasn't right inside my chest. Besides, whatever the ill-defined feeling was, it had already vanished, along with the clammy skin sensations. I felt almost normal. Maybe it was something else. Not my heart. Something not so serious. Something not so dangerous.

Who was I kidding? I couldn't run.

I continued to walk. I recalled the fainting spell at home six months earlier, when I had to focus hard as I reached the top of the stairs. I leaned on the handrail, concerned I might black out. After the feeling passed, I had the thought: I don't want to know what that was.

As I walked my workout route, I considered what to say to Kathy. I decided to wait until after a visit to Doctor Edelstein when I knew for sure what the hell was going on.

I drove to work a little earlier than usual to get out of the house before Kathy returned from driving the kids to school. I called the doctor from the office and got myself squeezed in for an appointment the next day, which was Friday.

"Then I had to stop running," I said to Doctor Edelstein, as I faced him across his desk.

"Tired? Exhausted?" Edelstein asked calmly, sounding almost blasé, his pen poised, hovering over the chart open before him.

I leaned in. "No, this wasn't normal," I said. "I literally couldn't run. Like my body just completely shut down."

"Well, let's do an EKG," Edelstein said, not appearing unduly concerned behind his thick, black-framed glasses. Perhaps that was understandable. After all, we were the same age, he didn't exercise, and he had the beginnings of a stoop. Plus, his practice was primarily geriatrics. Sick people in their 70s, 80s, and 90s had surrounded me in his waiting room, wobbling around with their healthcare aids and elderly spouses, or accompanied by what I took to be dutiful offspring. By comparison, I must have appeared awfully healthy to the sedentary doctor; plus, he knew I'd run marathons.

A female technician wheeled an EKG cart into the small examination room where I sat on the edge of the exam table, clad in my underwear under a flimsy disposable paper hospital gown. She was burly, blondish, wore a white smock, and spoke with a thick Eastern European accent.

"Remove the gown," she ordered, "and lay down."

I complied. She applied small glops of cold goop to my skin and hooked me up to about a dozen rubber suction pads with their wires leading to her portable machine. As I lay on my back and she administered the test, I thought that when I returned to Doctor Edelstein's office, I had to convince him how serious things were, change his blasé reaction and get him solving the crisis at hand.

I caught the technician frown as the machine ground out a sheet of paper.

"Something wrong?" I said.

"You can talk to the doctor about it," she responded brusquely. Then, she removed the wires and the suction pads and pointed to a roll of paper towels. "You can clean up and meet with the doctor back in his office," she said and left with her cart and the printout. I stood up, cleaned off the goop with paper towels, got dressed, and walked down the hallway to do battle with Doctor Edelstein.

Again, I faced him across the desk. His demeanor had changed completely; his face appeared ashen and stunned, and when he spoke, his voice caught in his throat.

"Your EKG is very out of the ordinary," he said, staring at the printout. "This is last year's result from your annual physical"— and he pushed both the previous year's printout and the new one across his desk, side-by-side.

"See," he said, using a pen to point out the disparity between the two sets of results. "The old graph line is smooth with a regular repeated pattern, while the new one"—and here, he ran his pen along herky-jerky lines with their abrupt, steep highs and lows— "indicates cardiac irregularity and could be blockage of an artery. I'm going to set you up with a cardiologist."

I sank back in the chair, speechless. I'd returned to his office to do battle, and now my worst fears had become his.

Doctor Edelstein stood up. "I'm sorry," he said, not looking me in the eye, as if thinking out loud or speaking to himself. "I should have been more aggressive treating your cholesterol, given you more tests, put you on a treadmill." He stepped out from behind the desk. "I'm going to call a cardiologist. I'll be right back."

He returned a few minutes later. "The appointment is for Monday morning," and he handed me a piece of paper with a time and name and address on it. "Take it easy over the weekend," he cautioned, "especially when going up stairs. And no running, of course. This is very serious."

I got up, and we said awkward good-byes—me not wanting him to feel any worse than he already did, in an apparent moment of crisis regarding his medical competency. I went out to my car, drove up Rodeo Drive with its high-end stores, across Santa Monica Boulevard, and past Beverly Hills mansions. Reaching Sunset Boulevard, I turned up Coldwater Canyon where at the top I headed east on Mulholland Drive with its nature-preserved land up above Fryman Canyon. There were views out over the San Fernando Valley that I enjoyed on my Sunday morning runs on the path beside the road. The views were meaningless today as I thought about what I would say to Kathy.

I didn't think, "Why me?" Why not me?

I turned left and drove down Laurel Canyon Boulevard and arrived at our house, where I found Kathy in the master bedroom, relaxing on the bed and watching a show on the Food Network. Today was a day off for her from working two 12-hour shifts a week as a pediatric bone marrow transplant nurse at Children's Hospital in Hollywood. The kids were still at school.

"How come you aren't at the office?" she said.

I sat down on the bed.

"What's wrong?"

"I—," I choked up. I couldn't get the words out. I hadn't expected this. While I was driving home, I had rehearsed what I would say. I had been smooth, calm, and in control during our imagined conversation.

"What is it?" she said, sitting up, alarmed.

"I just had an EKG," I managed to get out, tears coming. "It's my heart . . . a blockage maybe . . . something really serious. I've been having problems running." And I told her what had been going on.

We hugged, and she cried along with me.

"Why didn't you tell me?"

"I didn't want to alarm you. And I wanted to know for sure, first."

"I'm not done with you yet," she said softly. Then, she went into her organized, medically trained crisis mode—cautioning me to go up the stairs very slowly, asking questions about exactly what Doctor Edelstein had said, and saying that she would go to the cardiologist with me.

That night, we huddled with Cassidy and Jamie and explained what we knew so far. There were tears and hugs.

CHAPTER 13

RANGER RICK

I continued running down from Skeleton Point, savoring the solitude. Just like I relished my Sunday-run solitude on the hillside trails back in Los Angeles, where I'd sometimes spot a scurrying rabbit, a skittering lizard, a mule deer in the brush, a retreating coyote, or even a snake. Snakes, especially large black Southern Pacific rattlers, sometimes sunned themselves on the exposed area of a trail. There was excitement at a sighting of these fascinating creatures, going back to my early childhood and time spent in the woods behind our house in New Jersey, where I sought refuge and encounters with nature: white-tailed deer, box turtles, water life in a stream that ran through it. Back then, when it came to snakes, I found nothing more exotic than the benign, commonplace garter variety, although even that was exciting to me.

My girls called me Ranger Rick when they were younger—or perhaps I'd bestowed that mantle upon myself, and they just humored me by repeating it. I'd take them to find tadpoles in the streams and the temporary pond that formed in Franklin Canyon during the rainy season, and to look for snakes.

One hot summer day in Los Angeles, Cassidy and I had gone hiking up the Viewcrest Trail near our house in search of a rattlesnake sighting. Just as we neared the junction with the main fire trail and were feeling it was not our day, there it was: a good four feet or more in length, thick, with black patterns separated by light bands—the markings of a venomous Southern Pacific Rattlesnake. At first, it curled up and shook the rattle at the end of its tail, as we kept our distance just out of its striking range. Then, it took off, slithering away quickly. We followed until it disappeared into the thick brush. A perfect Dad/daughter adventure.

When I ran in the hills, I watched out for snakes and was careful to avoid stepping on a too-slow-to-move lizard. In the spring, following the rainy season, I reveled in the bright yellow wildflowers that blossomed alongside the Ridge Trail in a chest-high golden path. It was as if I was parting them as I ran, and sometimes I was—my shoulders pushing them aside, having to dodge the tallest ones, brushing against my face, surrounding me with their radiant beauty—.

Shit!

Two guys, side by side, came into view on the SK, a few hundred yards below, descending the switchbacks at a good clip. They weren't young. In fact, the two of them with gray hair peeking out from under, respectively, a baseball cap and an Australian bush hat, weren't much older than I was—if they were older at all.

How had they gotten so far in front of me? Maybe they'd parked in one of the spaces along the rim road that you had to arrive early to snag, and then hiked into the trailhead. They didn't have backpacks, only daypacks, so they likely weren't in one of the limited parking spots at Yaki Point for those with camping permits or reservations in one of the overnight cottages booked at Phantom Ranch. Rather, they had the look of in-shape day hikers.

My competitive instincts kicked in. I couldn't help myself. I formulated plans to pass them. I looked for a place with extra room up ahead, as we switch-backed down the SK to the fast-approaching Tonto. It was like when I spotted someone who I thought could be in my age group during the annual Kennebunkport Day at the Beach 5K, late in the race with everything on the line. I'd been blessed with a kick as a miler in high school. I could still employ it to pick off pretty much anyone who looked to be a potential threat in the closing few hundred yards of a race. That final burst of speed could make the difference between placing second, third, or first. In the 2008 Kennebunkport 5K, I'd kicked past a grey-haired guy in a red cap, giving it my all to make sure I was ahead of him. I'd passed him with just yards to go as the digital finish clock ticked off our times and won my age group.

But today in the Canyon, I wasn't in a race against anyone, not officially anyway. There was only the clock ticking inside my head. Still, I picked up my pace and started closing the distance. The switchbacks here were free of cross-trail logs, the trail fast, if steep.

I spotted a mule train making its way up toward us.

Damn.

The two men ahead of me were talking, glancing at the mule train, and obviously didn't hear me approaching. I reached them just as they moved off the trail at a switchback, and I pulled off the trail behind them, the mule train closer now. A lone rider on a horse led the mules. He held a rein in one hand and, with the other, a rope strung from the lead mule. Hooves thudding, dust kicking up, the eight or ten animals followed behind, single file, roped together. They went by us as we stood aside, their heads nodding in unison, each mule carrying bulky oversized bags of what I presumed to be trash from Phantom Ranch.

After the last mule passed, the two men left the switchback and returned to the trail in front of me.

"Excuse me," I announced. One of them turned and gave me an annoyed look. Then, they stopped and moved over as I went by. I picked up speed, heading down the switchbacks—a mixture of pale beige and gray limestone rocks around me; a powdery, white dirt path before me.

CHAPTER 14

THE WIDOW-MAKER

FEBRUARY 5, 2007

It looked like a bomb had gone off in my artery. Kathy and I stared at the black-and-white image on the monitor. At the point of the occlusion, chunks of plaque were jumbled like a pile of boulders in a tunnel cave-in.

"You should have suffered a major myocardial infarction on your run—a massive heart attack, in layman's terms," Doctor Lewis said matter-of-factly. We were in his hospital office four days after my visit with Doctor Edelstein. "Which," Doctor Lewis added," would have been fatal unless you were in close proximity to emergency medical assistance with shock paddles applied immediately to your chest. Even then, it's hard to say that you could have been saved. Your LAD——that's the left anterior descending artery, which carries 50% of the blood circulating from your heart—is completely occluded. Possibly due to plaque that ruptured."

"But I eat pretty healthy, and I don't smoke," I said.

"Sometimes plaque production is just genetic. You do have that pulmonary history in your family on your mother's side. You didn't suffer that massive heart attack because of these," the cardiologist said, moving closer to the monitor and pointing to the black-and-white image of the CT scan. Then, he ran a fingertip across the screen and a network of small blood vessels in the vicinity of the blockage. "We call these collateral blood vessels. They're created by the heart to pump more blood and respond to the rigors of your distance running. They managed to carry just enough blood around the blockage to spare you from that massive heart attack."

I peered at the impossibly small filaments and pictured myself dead on a run, genetically programmed to die at 59.

"So, running saved my life," I said.

"Yes, you could say that."

Kathy and I shared a look. Years earlier, while strolling through our old neighborhood in Hollywood, I'd felt the need to sit down and rest on a low wall. At the time, Kathy asked me if anything was wrong. I replied that I wasn't sure. But concerned about my health, I returned to running for the first time in a decade, and I hadn't stopped since.

Doctor Lewis continued, "I should add you also have an 80% blockage of the smaller circumflex artery, which carries an additional 10% of your blood." He pointed out the vessel on the CT scan, and a portion where the artery almost disappeared due to the blockage, as if cut in two with only a small strand connecting the two halves. "You did also suffer some damage from the myocardial infarction—a mild heart attack. I estimate you lost about 10% of your heart muscle."

"Jesus. So, where do we go from here?"

"We'll try an angioplasty to break up the main blockage and place three stents to open up your LAD here, here, and here," the cardiologist said, noting the locations on the screen. "We can deal with the smaller circumflex occlusion later with a second angioplasty. As for the main blockage, it's quite severe. An angioplasty may not work. In that case, we'll need to do open-heart bypass surgery. I do have to warn you that either surgery carries a risk. Small, but possibly fatal—except in your case, because it's a complete occlusion, the risk is higher. After you sign the paperwork, I have an operating room booked Wednesday. In the meantime, don't do anything strenuous. Even take stairs slow and easy."

We reviewed the forms. I deferred to Kathy and her medical expertise as an RN.

On our way out of the building, Kathy said, "Do you know what they call the left anterior descending artery?"

"No," I said.

"The widow-maker."

CHAPTER 15

PANGAEA REDUX: EXTINCTION AS THE WAY OF LIFE

For all of its fantastical, primal allure, Pangaea was no Garden of Eden. Two of the five major mass extinctions that have taken place on Earth occurred on Pangaea and in the surrounding Panthalassa Ocean. The Third Extinction, the greatest mass extinction event in the history of the planet, took place about 250 million years ago on the supercontinent and came close to wiping out all life on earth. Seventy percent of land animals and 95 percent of marine life disappeared. The Third Extinction was followed, fifty million years later, by the Fourth Extinction, also on Pangaea. It may have been tied to the breakup of the huge landmass and resulting climate change as ocean currents shifted and Greenland's new ice sheet helped to cool the Earth.

At the end of the Mesozoic Era, Earth experienced its fifth and, to date, last extinction—100 million-plus years after the disintegration of Pangaea: The Cretaceous-Paleogene Extinction Event a.k.a K-T Extinction. Three quarters of all species were wiped out by a six-mile-wide asteroid slamming into Earth 66 million years ago, creating the Chicxulub Crater in the Yucatan Peninsula on the southeastern coast of Mexico. The crater was 110 miles in diameter and 12 miles deep. The impact displaced 40,000 cubic miles of dirt and sediment, the equivalent to a million H-bombs exploding, as day turned to night from the debris tossed up into the atmosphere and temperatures plunged.

Most famously, the Fifth Extinction ended the Age of the Dinosaurs, the dominant species on Earth for about 200 million years. Most birds and reptiles were also lost, and about two-thirds of mammal species. Overall, 75 percent of species were eradicated, including the Ammonites, like the one preserved as the fossil I found on that family vacation. After floating in the world's oceans for more than *300 million years* in their elaborate, nautilus-like spiral shells, they were all—more than 10,000 different species—wiped out as the seas turned toxic. The fossil record shows that some survived for a time in the Western Interior Seaway—a body of water that once split the continent of North America—before those stragglers also died out.

In her compelling book *The Sixth Extinction*, author Elizabeth Kolbert makes the case that we are now living through the next extinction event. A supporting photo of a dozen dead mountain yellow-legged frogs, scattered, bloated and belly-up on rocks in a stream, is disturbing—amphibians being the species most sensitive to climate change and a leading indicator of disaster. Reef-building corals, freshwater mollusks, sharks, a quarter of all mammals, a fifth of reptiles, and a sixth of birds are fast disappearing. The difference this time is that man may be causing the catastrophe or, at minimum, compounding it.

The Grand Canyon wasn't in existence for any of the past extinctions, only the current one. The Canyon was once thought to have been created 10 million years ago, long after the end of the Kaibab seas, when a tectonic uplift of the Colorado Plateau and the corrosive power of the Colorado River combined to create perhaps Earth's most majestic feature. More recent research has pushed back the formation of the Canyon to potentially 17 million years ago, the process of erosion starting perhaps as far back as 40 million years.

Of course, people weren't around to witness any of the past extinctions—or to be wiped out. The oldest fossils of humans, or more correctly our non-human apelike precursors, come from the Rift Valley in Kenya, specifically a cave that served as living quarters and shelter for a group of Australopithecus dated at about 4.1 million years ago. But Homo sapiens—us—go back a mere few hundred thousand years.

Life on Earth is in a state of constant change. Depending on which source you use, 90 to 99.9% of all species that existed on the planet are now extinct.

I had faced my own extinction, not at some vague indeterminant future time, but at the shocking age of 59.

CHAPTER 16

YOUR ANGIOPLASTY WILL BE TELEVISED

FEBRUARY 7, 2007

Sick people surrounded me on gurneys in pre-op. People cocooned in the unhealthy-looking skin of lifelong smokers, people severely overweight, people years older than me. I lay on my own gurney, clad in a pale hospital gown, wearing only my underwear underneath, stripped of my BlackBerry, cell phone, wallet, keys—all taken away in a bag of personal possessions along with my clothes and shoes. Kathy stood nearby, protective, running interference for me with the medical staff. The girls were in the care of friends for the drive to school and afterwards. There had been some tears, but they took their cues from Kathy and me as we tried to put on a positive front.

An IV protruded out of the back of my hand with clear tubing running up to a pole attached to the gurney, where an inverted plastic bag drained fluid. The anesthesiologist came by and administered the sedative through a port in the IV and imparted surprising news: "This won't knock you out," he said. "You can either go to sleep or stay awake during the angioplasty."

I immediately resolved to stay conscious to find out as soon as possible whether the angioplasty was successful, or whether I would need to have my chest cracked for open-heart surgery with all the added risk and weeks instead of days of recovery.

A male attendant in light blue scrubs appeared and rolled me on my gurney out of pre-op and down a hallway with Kathy at my side. We arrived at large, closed double-doors. Kathy bent over me and whispered, "I love you, I love you, I love you," and I repeated it back to her. Then, the attendant punched the button on the wall, the gurney penetrated the big double doors, and we were separated. The guy wheeled me down a short hallway and into a room where he delivered me parallel to an operating table.

"Can you scooch over?" he said.

I moved over and onto the operating table. I lifted my head and peered at a pair of TV screens that were V-flanged at a wide angle, perhaps 10 feet beyond my toes. I had a clear view of one of them. I realized if I kept myself from going under, the proximity and angle of the screen would permit me to watch my own angioplasty—televised.

"Yes, you can watch the fluoroscopy as they work," the attendant said, as if reading my mind. "Good luck," he added, and he left. I was alone in the room with my thoughts. The anesthesia was having a sedating, calming effect, and I focused my mind on staying conscious rather than on my life hanging in the balance.

Doctor Lewis entered the room in scrubs.

"Are we okay?" he said.

"Ready when you are," I answered gamely.

"Doctor Johnson will be assisting me," he said, as another man in scrubs entered the room. A nurse joined them. "First, we need to insert a cardiac catheter into your thigh and go into the femoral artery," Doctor Lewis added. "It'll serve as the angioplasty access point."

I lay on the operating table and willed myself to stay conscious as they set up the cardiac catheter near my groin. In short order, Doctor Lewis went to work on the angioplasty itself, operating hand controls, the assisting doctor beside him. The two of them stared at the screens, manipulating the thin wire through the large catheter needle protruding from my thigh, then running it up through up my blood vessels until it reached the blocked artery. The doctors gazed intently at the image of the occlusion; I also watched their efforts as I fought the effects of the anesthesia.

I saw the wire reach the blockage as the doctors pierced, probed, and roto-rootered the occlusion. They spoke occasionally to each other, working in tandem in the soft glow of the screens. Since Doctor Lewis had warned me the blockage was severe, I had the thought that the longer they kept working, the better—the more likely the angioplasty procedure would be successful and the less likely I would be subjected to open-heart surgery.

As I stayed glued to their efforts, I saw the blockage begin to break up. A feeling of relief surged through me. The angioplasty was becoming almost routine as I watched them work.

Doctor Lewis turned back to me. "Congratulations," he said." It's been successful. Now we're going to place the stents."

I relaxed. My life would go on. The kids would not be left without a father. Kathy would not be left to struggle on alone.

I was out of the woods—or so I thought.

That night in my hospital room, with Kathy guardedly agreeing to it, I walked into the bathroom under the effects of morphine I'd been given post-op. I pulled my IV drip pole beside me on its moveable stand as I moved slowly, unhooked from the cardiac monitor, my thumb unclipped from the pulse oximeter device that recorded the oxygen saturation of my blood.

As I stood in front of the toilet and tried to urinate, I collapsed dead away to the floor, but somehow missed striking my head against the metal toilet. I came to, my face flush against the floor, staring back into the room to see Kathy rushing to my side. She pushed the emergency button on the wall as I struggled to get up, and she helped me back to the bed as I leaned on her strong shoulders. Kathy was yelling towards the doorway: "He coded!" Then, "Where's the crash cart?!? He's had a syncopal episode!"

Kathy hooked me back up to the monitors. As I lay on the bed, barely conscious, I looked over at the flashing red numbers and saw my heart rate climbing back out of the fatal 20s to the 30s, 40s, and the 50s, the blood pressure numbers also recovering.

Meanwhile, Kathy was out in the hallway shouting instructions, taking charge, putting her own RN experience to use, and getting into it with an inexperienced nurse who didn't understand the dire situation.

The crisis was exacerbated, because I'd been moved from the ICU post-op recovery unit that had been closed due to an insufficient number of patients. I was now in a regular wing of the hospital, without a crash cart and its emergency medical equipment and supplies or specially trained personnel, and no oxygen at the bedside.

Additional staff arrived from the nurses' station, alerted by the alarm. Kathy called Doctor Lewis. "I don't believe it," she reported back. "He wouldn't come to the hospital, because he wasn't on call."

It was determined that I was allergic to morphine—the reason for my collapse. Meanwhile, urine kept building up in my bladder. I was unable to relieve myself, although I tried to do it into a bedpan. The size of my distended bladder was heading to dangerous proportions as an ultrasound brought into check it revealed that retention was up to 900ccs, about a quart.

"We'll need to insert a rubber catheter into your penis," said a nurse, after she and Kathy talked.

"There's no other choice?" I asked.

"No."

"It's going to be painful," Kathy said.

The pain of the catheter being inserted into my penis was excruciating—unbearable really, and the most pain I'd ever been through in my life. I screamed and yelled as Kathy gripped my hands. The catheter was finally inserted; urine began draining into a clear bag at my bedside. After the room had cleared of nurses and support staff, the potentially fatal emergency averted, Kathy told me about my collapse in the bathroom. "Your face was blue and your lips were gray," she said.

I'd come closer to death in the hospital room than on the operating table.

CHAPTER 17

TRAVERSING THE TONTO

I was running on the Tonto Platform, surrounded by the pervasive blackbrush scrub. The Tonto stretched from the base of the South Rim to the top of the river gorge. While nearly flat in some spots, it was largely an uneven topography of slopes, mini-hills, eroded ravines, and side-canyons, crossed in places by seasonal streams.

The geological stratum was the Tonto Group: Muav Limestone on top, then Bright Angel Shale, and Tapeats Sandstone. The shale, with its greenish tint, was the main component of the Tonto and about 500 feet thick. The three layers combined for more than 1,000 feet before reaching the Vishnu Schist that was the basement rock of the Canyon. If you had come to this area 515 million years ago at the cusp between the Muay Limestone and the Bright Angel Shale, you'd have found another warm, shallow, muddy sea, this one full of primitive trilobites and brachiopods.

I hit another patch of cross-trail logs, the going rough, and I returned to cadence-counting until I reached a brief section that was paved with stones and led to a smoother part of the route.

Directly ahead and across the way, the North Rim grew closer. I could see, with increasing clarity, the complex of rising buttes, bluffs, and mesas that projected outward, the colors and features becoming more defined as the day became brighter. I was able to distinguish the herky-jerky line of the ravine above Phantom Ranch that was home to Bright Angel Creek and the North Kaibab Trail. I could see where the Clear Creek Trail headed east, up past Sumner Butte to the Ottoman Amphitheater, a vast open expanse at 4,500 feet. Further to the east was Cape Royal, Freya Castle, Angel's Gate, and more exotically named landmarks: Wotan's Throne, Jupiter Temple, and, higher up, the Rama and Krishna Shrines, and the striking Vishnu Temple, a dramatic pyramid of rock that rose 7,500 feet above Vishnu Canyon. To the west of Phantom Ranch were more landmarks: Cheops Pyramid at 5,000 feet, Osiris Temple at 6,600 feet, Isis Temple at 7,000 feet, and the Tower of Ra, a picturesque butte, at just over 6,000 feet.

I supposed the names, if not religious, were in keeping with the spiritual nature and wonder of the Canyon. So must have thought geologist Clarence Dutton whose work after the Civil War laid the groundwork for an understanding of how the Canyon was formed. Dutton believed the Grand Canyon was such an impressive and important feature that it should reflect mythologies and religions from around the world. Therefore, he named many of these features accordingly in his *Tertiary History of the Grand Canon District* study of the Grand Canyon, published in 1882.

THE TIP OFF

I cruised onto the Tip Off, the last of the three landmark open spaces on the South Kaibab Trail, following Cedar Ridge and Skeleton Point. It was a wide-open expanse of brown, powdered dirt with low rocks lining the trail through it. Two signs were connected at right angles atop each other and affixed to a short, stout

The Tip Off

post, a jumble of rocks surrounding its base. The topmost one said, "TIP OFF," and the one below it, "TONTO TRAIL." The Tonto's thin strip of dirt intersected on my left and right.

This was where Margaret Bradley would have connected into the South Kaibab from the Tonto Trail, arriving from the east— had she made it. And this was where her companion Ryan did make it when he struggled in from the Tonto and started yelling for help after the emergency phone didn't work.

I had the Tip Off to myself, like it had been deserted for Ryan. I hadn't seen anyone since I passed the two older guys. I paused, had a drink of water, and dropped my daypack. I felt strangely vulnerable standing there alone at the site of Ryan's dehydrated desperation; it would have been about this time of the morning.

Someday, I would like to run or hike a section of the Tonto. Traversed by few, with no reliable year-round water, it was far more daunting than the SK and Bright Angel. There were plenty of warnings about the lesser-used trail: flashfloods, lack of water, the danger of extreme heat and dehydration. Hikers or runners

     RICK MATER

who ventured onto the desolate Tonto found themselves in challenging, even perilous isolation and engulfed by brutal temperatures during the summer.

I especially wanted to make it to Cremation Creek and pay my respects to Margaret Bradley. Dying alone on a run that had started out as demanding but doable for a young, confident athlete.

You just never knew when your life could be over without warning.

CHAPTER 18

A RUNNER ONCE MORE

To my surprise, I was discharged the day after the angioplasty despite the post-op emergency. Doctor Lewis phoned it in, literally—calling the hospital with the order to send me home. Only Doctor Edelstein came by to look in on me. Kathy arrived at my room early in the morning and drove me home that afternoon. On our way, we picked up the girls who had been visiting with friends from school.

Two days later, on Saturday, I dragged myself off the couch in the family room, having watched too much TV. Despite it not being ordinary for a patient to exercise so soon after the procedure, I was undeterred. I didn't feel fully recovered, but I put on my running shoes and jeans anyway and headed out the door after alerting Kathy.

"Just taking a short exercise walk," I said.

"Okay," she answered, "but please take it easy."

At her insistence, I had a slip of paper with my name, address, and home phone number in a pocket, and I carried my cell phone. Had I required open-heart surgery, I would still be flat on my back in the hospital—and that's assuming everything went well. Instead, I walked the familiar route at a good clip in the crisp morning air.

A few hundred yards from the house, I turned right onto Laurel Canyon Boulevard. Slipping between the row of slender conifers that signaled the change from sidewalk concrete to dirt path, I continued briskly past the spot of my cardiac disaster. Nine days after my heart attack occurred here and three days after the emergency angioplasty, I was back walking along Fryman Road, doing my regular three-mile route at a comfortable pace. There was no sidewalk here, just the paved street, the spacious houses, plentiful trees, and a meadow where deer sometimes came down from the hills during the dry season to eat the grass.

I made the turn onto Iredell Street, walking past more of the large homes. I heard a "rat-tat-tat" against a tree, followed by the sharp trill of a Nutall's woodpecker; the copycat call of a mocking-bird; the "keree-keree" of a red-tailed hawk—there it was, perched majestic in a tall Eucalyptus tree.

It was all a shimmery wonder to behold, almost hallucinogenic. I was experiencing the world as if I had been born into it anew. Could this state of wonder at being alive continue? Could I be for-ever changed? Perhaps a new outlook on life would lift me above the trivial day-to-day BS. The bad days at the job; the time spent thinking about the next career move; never being satisfied enough with corporate achievement as a yardstick of meaningful accom-plishment to begin with.

Could every day instead become a gift to be treasured?

"I think it's time to hang up your running shoes," Doctor Lewis said, without looking up as he sat at a desk filling out my chart. It was my angioplasty follow-up visit, five days after the procedure and two days after my rapturous return to Fryman Canyon. I sat in a chair across from him, Kathy sitting next to me.

"Maybe some light jogging for 20 minutes a day," he contin-ued. "Three days a week, tops. Nothing more than that."

I was stunned. "But running saved my life. You admitted as much yourself. And perhaps those collateral blood vessels will atrophy without it?" I said, trying to martial a medical argument.

"I can't sign off on it. Running is a risk factor now," the doctor said, with a momentary lift of his head in my direction. "For another heart attack. Maybe a stroke."

Kathy turned to me. "I think we should get a second opinion," she said.

"Well, that's certainly your right," Doctor Lewis replied, seeming to not particularly care one way or another.

Kathy and I found another cardiologist, one who was experienced in sports medicine. I quickly made an appointment. Doctor Stephens turned out to be an avid cyclist and reviewed the angioplasty material contained on a CD Kathy had smartly thought to get from the hospital.

"Keep me posted on the progress of your walking, and we'll talk about easing into doing some hills," Doctor Stephens told me. "And move from there to running, if everything goes well."

"Absolutely," I said. "What about the second angioplasty?"

"I don't know that it's worth going into that circumflex artery."

I wanted to cheer at the news that I wouldn't have another angioplasty but wondered about the impact of the blockage on my body, including my running.

"What about the loss of 10% of my blood circulation?" I asked. "And Doctor Lewis told me that I also lost about 10% of my heart muscle."

"Well, I'm not sure the percentages are quite that high. Let's focus on sensibly moving forward."

"That's great," I said.

Day 17 after my angioplasty, I wore my running shoes, shorts, and a T-shirt, carried the who-I-was-should-I-drop-dead information slip in a pocket and my cell phone in a hand, ready to go for my Sunday workout. I'd been walking short routes near the house. Before heading out, I checked myself on the portable digital device that I now used to monitor my blood pressure at home. I strapped the cuff around my arm and hit "Start." With a humming noise from the equipment, the cuff crackled as it tightened against my right bicep while I watched the machine's window for readings until the numbers locked in: 120 over 80, my pulse 51—low for most people, but typical for me due to my running. After each exercise walk, I'd check the numbers again.

I went out the front door, going up Laurel Canyon. Past the Fryman Canyon turn, I took a left and hiked the steepest side street that I knew. I reached Mulholland Drive after powering up the curving route at a brisk pace, turned right, and headed west, walking along the edge of the road with views out over the San Fernando Valley. The sun was shining brightly. As I took in my surroundings, so familiar yet so new to me since the angioplasty, I thought, *"I can't believe I might never have been up here again."*

I started to jog down the gentle S-curve of the road, ignoring that I was ahead of Doctor Stephens' moderate walking-only schedule. I checked my watch. After five minutes of easy jogging, I resumed walking, continuing to head west on Mulholland. After 20 minutes, I took off again, mixing running with hiking breaks on my way to what would become a seven-mile workout. Feeling good, feeling really good.

I was a runner once more!

CHAPTER 19

RUNNING THE GREAT ARC

At the Tip Off, I took a sip of bottled water and placed the partially drained container inside my daypack. I wanted to keep my hands free for the Great Arc. I picked up the daypack and continued past the Tonto Trail junction at an easy trot, a horse-and-mule metal hitching post on my right. Just past the hitching post, I noticed an old, hard-to-read wooden sign, chest-high on a tilted post that appeared as if it was in danger of falling over. I thought that this sign was how they all should look in the Grand Canyon: timeless, weathered, hinting at danger—as if you were in the Old West and putting everything at risk. I paused for a closer look. The sign said:

"S KAIBAB TRAIL
TIP OFF
EMERGENCY PHONE"

This must be the phone that didn't work for Ryan that July morning. Behind the sign, I could make out a couple of poles askew with a wire strung between them. The phone was there

somewhere in the thick brush. I glimpsed a little path up the hillside and wondered if the phone was working now.

Past the emergency phone, the top of the river gorge was visible
up ahead. The trail disappeared over the edge as the SK began a
long descent to the river. I maintained a good pace as I ran alongside a deepening ravine on my left and an uphill slope on my right.
Cross-trail logs re-appeared, the dirt in between them gouged by
erosion, and the going quickly became tough. Then, the way was
briefly paved with rough stones as a switchback cut sharply right.

Up ahead, a giant sweeping curve of trail greeted me and plum-
meted into the gorge. Bright red dirt cascaded down alongside the
route where the trail was etched against a small, reddish butte. A
Canyon blogger had christened this stretch of the South Kaibab
the "Great Arc." I'd never seen the Great Arc spelled out on any
map but thought that it was the perfect name for this graceful seg-
ment of the SK's long, final dive to the Colorado.

On my practice hike, I'd spotted a small figure heading up the
Great Arc as if to meet me—a lone individual hunched over hiking poles and weighted down by a large backpack. I'd proceeded
down at a cautious jog, testing things out for running the Canyon.
Watching my feet, I noticed my white sweat socks were quickly
covered in red dust.

The figure became clearer as the distance between us tightened. Upon closer inspection, I realized it was a woman. As I approached, I guessed her to be about my age, perhaps a few years
older. She wore a rust-colored T-shirt, old dark shorts, and hiking
boots, the large backpack rising over her head. She took measured
steps up the SK, moving methodically.

My old running shoes with their worn threads had trouble
gripping the gravelly sand. My left shoe skidded, and my hands
flew up in the air as I struggled for balance. Regaining my footing,
I took an inside track on the trail, hugging the hillside to avoid

the drop on my left. My left foot skidded once more, and again I recovered my balance as I reached the woman.

"Whoa. Better slow down, partner," she said, pausing, leaning on her hiking poles.

I paused also. "Yes, I think maybe I'd better."

"Nothing the matter with just walking it," the woman said, gazing up at me. She had a ruddy, lined face, like she'd been hiking in the sun for years.

"Actually, I'm testing running the Canyon."

She examined my face. "Why?"

"I'm going to see if I can do it under six hours—down to Phantom Ranch and back up."

"Yeah, but why?"

"Well, it's a long story." I didn't want to get into the cardiac issues. Life and death. What doctors were telling me that I could and could not do.

"That's not what I meant," she said. "Why are you *running* through all of this?" She raised one of her hiking poles and indicated the grandeur of the Canyon all around us.

I stood there, uncertain how to respond.

"I hope you aren't planning on coming back up this way," she said. "Wouldn't recommend it."

"You're doing it."

"I'm a desert rat. Come here every year from Victorville. Done this and many other routes. Hike, take in the beauty, camp, meditate in my own way. Guess you could say I commune with nature. Me and the Canyon, we have a special relationship. I respect her and go with the flow where the trails lead me."

"That's great," I said.

"There's no rush is what I'm saying. You aren't exactly a youngster." She squinted and continued. "With age comes wisdom, don't they say?"

I laughed. "I suppose. Well, it's time to get going. Nice chatting!" I started walking, but after a couple dozen yards, I tried out more running. Below the last of the huge, graceful curve, the trail became less slippery. Then, thinking about what the woman had said, I slowed, went back to walking, and looked back. I saw her small again, making her way up the trail with her hiking poles, the burden of the backpack still hunching her over as she took her deliberate steps.

Today as I ran the Great Arc for real, the trail steepened and looped down in front of me. There was no one else in sight. I mostly made good time—cross-trail logs either submerged or gone completely, the water breaks only occasional. At a series of curves, things became more challenging, the logs more prominent. I had to keep an eye on my footing.

At a sharp switchback, I could see the rest of the trail snaking back and forth, the Black Bridge spanning the Colorado below and visible for the first time. I was surrounded by soaring rock formations as I ran. There were buttes on both sides of the river, scattered low scrub around me. Across the way on the North Rim were the tops of the temples: Brahma, Buddha, and Manu, poking their spires above the surrounding terrain like majestic guideposts.

THE GREAT UNCONFORMITY

Below the Great Arc, where the Tapeats Sandstone rested atop the Vishnu Schist, was the Great Unconformity. Here the orderly horizontal layers of strata—neatly piled on each other and marked by their different colors and textures, from the top of the South Rim down—came to an abrupt end. The Great Unconformity represented hundreds of millions of years of geological history gone missing, most likely due to massive erosion from oceans and inland seas.

The terrain here told the story of Pannotia, the supercontinent that existed before Pangaea. Pannotia had begun to break up and drift apart about 550 million years ago. The rocks around me also gave evidence of Rodinia, the supercontinent before Pannotia, from over a *billion* years ago. Rodinia, which had consisted of endless miles of barren ground before life appeared on land, was ripped apart 750 million years ago, following a rift that was thought to have formed a few hundred miles to the west of the Canyon, where Death Valley is today.

Everything below the Great Unconformity was off-kilter, full of faults, layers at sharp angles, and disorganized sections of hardened primal sediment. The geological record here became something of a cypher, open to speculation. In fact, the closer to the bottom of the Canyon you got, the more scientific study of the surrounding rocks reflected an amalgam of analysis and *guesswork*. Mystery replaced certainty, with as many questions raised as answered. Like the questions I increasingly put to myself about my life and its many contradictions. Those paths taken and not taken; idealism gained and lost.

Before the time recounted in my novel *Beat*, there was everything that came before it in the late 1960s and early 1970s. Events, decisions, and actions taken that seemed to have a moral clarity attached in those times of political and personal turmoil—but at a cost. I hadn't always been so clear about wanting to live as I was today, barring something as profoundly disturbing as Alzheimer's upending everything.

#STUDENT REVOLUTIONARY: COUNTERCULTURE AWAKENING—1968

One day, my college roommate and I moved an old bookcase in the little living room of our funky off-campus apartment. We discovered that it had masked a fist-sized hole in the wall. Graffiti around the hole read "Pad North," and there were cryptic signatures, some nicked from the book and movie *Gidget*: The Big Kahuna, Moondoggie, and Lover Boy. It made that dump of a place feel special. "Pad North" was a remnant of the impact of the Beat Generation. We wondered if there'd also been Pads South, East, and West.

Beat poet Allen Ginsberg visited our Pennsylvania campus, playing his harmonium and reciting *Sunflower*, *Amerika*, and *Howl*. When he finished, we gathered around, eager acolytes, as he descended from the stage. I approached him, pulled out a joint, and said, "Wanna hit?" To my surprise—after all we were standing in the middle of the college auditorium, surrounded by a several hundred people—Ginsberg said, "Sure, man."

I lit up, took a toke, and passed him the joint. We stood there trading hits, me and Ginsberg. He shared the joint with others around us, and I invited him to come along with us to hang out at Pad North. He demurred, saying something about a commitment to a faculty gathering as a professor showed up to lead him away.

There was also a campus appearance by activist-writer Paul Krassner, reading from his satirical magazine, *The Realist*, and educating us about his idol, Lenny Bruce, and old lefty I.F. Stone. Krassner also took credit for concocting the hippie excogitation Yippie!—derived from Youth International Party, a coterie of political anarchist tricksters that included his pals Abbie Hoffman and Jerry Rubin.

By my sophomore year, I was smoking grass every night, experimenting with LSD, and trying other drugs as they came along. My cross-country team participation had ended due to a loss of interest, and despite the entreaties of my coach. Going out for track fell off the radar as well. My attendance in classes had become erratic; exams were a last-minute panic. After suffering through my first all-nighter on wretched vending-machine coffee, speed became my study aid of choice. On speed, textbooks were interesting; novels, personal odysseys of discovery; and literary masters, revelatory.

In short order, I wouldn't even consider an all-nighter without methamphetamine in some form. Prescription diet pills like Dexedrine were best. Speed worked wonders as long as you fought the urge to merely yammer to whomever chanced to pass by. In the end, you made it through the test, struggling to write down all the information spilling out of your brain, convinced you were doing just great. You settled for a "C"—if you were lucky.

I started to take speed even if there wasn't an exam to cram for. On a beautiful spring day, I read *Demian* on the green grass under the big, shady oak trees near the gymnasium, blissfully cutting classes, convinced I was learning more than I ever could if confined inside the stultifying classrooms of proscribed tutelage. I underlined passages and scribbled comments in the margins, relating what the book was telling me about life, about myself— finally learning something that mattered.

Soon, I was steeped in my own personal college syllabus: novels by Hesse, Burroughs, Genet; poetry by Ginsberg, Rimbaud, and Gary Snyder; philosophy from Sartre and Camus; radical works like *Soul on Ice* by Eldridge Cleaver, *Black Power* by Stokely Carmichael, and *Die Nigger Die!* by H. Rap Brown. Plus, there was pop-culture fluff like *The Strawberry Statement: Notes of a Campus Revolutionary* (a student radical admires the braless breasts beneath the T-shirts of his female co-revolutionaries); *The Gap* ("Peace? Pot? Protest? Pow!" blared the cover as, inside, an uncle and his Columbia University nephew recount a story of generational pseudo-conflict for 127 lightweight paperback pages); and more seriously, Richard Farina's acclaimed debut novel *Been*

   RICK MATER

Down So Long It Looks Like Up to Me, written before he was tragically killed in a motorcycle crash.

By my 21st birthday, I was on the verge of flunking out of school. It was my junior year, and I was wondering what the hell I was going to do if I lost my student draft deferment. My life wasn't at all how I'd expected it to turn out when I was in high school—a college-bound straight arrow on the debate team; features editor for the school newspaper; president of the political science and chess clubs; on the track, wresting, and cross-country teams. My high school career plans to go into State Department foreign service work had become a forgotten fantasy, the prospects of gaining the necessary security clearance dubious. With my SDS radical anti-war activities, I suspected I might already have an FBI file.

There was also my questionable mental state, with the lingering impact of sometimes harrowing acid trips and my participation in ever more violent anti-war demonstrations. My alienation from mainstream America had diminished any purpose to a college degree or career aspirations.

On my birthday, December 6, 1968, I sat on a metal folding chair at a rickety card table that doubled as a desk in Pad North. I lined up the pills and capsules that were an ancillary part of my pot stash and stared at them. There were amphetamines—a half-dozen oblong, white pills speckled with pale green, and bootleg White Crosses that could be anything from caffeine to meth. There were a few prescription Dexamyl and Dexedrine time-release capsules with their colorful tiny balls inside—reliable for last-minute speed-fueled all-nighters to cram for exams in classes I was only sporadically attending.

A few Valiums—yellow 5 mgs and blue 10 mgs—were also among the pills arrayed on the table, along with a number of other assorted tranquilizers and some barbiturates. They came in handy for coming down from acid at the end of a trip, especially if the

LSD was cut with speed and it was damned near impossible to go to sleep, no matter that you'd been up all night and were exhausted. There were even a couple of Thorazines in my stash, treasured as an emergency bailout to avoid the potential drive to a hospital if somebody was having a tough time of it while tripping.

I knew there were probably not enough pills to kill me, and only the downs were really useful. Or maybe an overdose from speed was possible? I wasn't sure. Besides, I would be looking for a peaceful end to it—not some fatal hyper-speed freak-out.

I hadn't yet realized that I suffered from bouts of depression. Not the stay-in-bed-all-day incapacitating kind, rather more a walking-around-able-to-function-if-need-be affliction. So there was that to contend with, plus losing my moorings—the security of my upper-middle-class upbringing stripped away in the craziness of the times.

A page in Camus' *The Myth of Sisyphus* lay open before me— with a passage underlined in red, about there being no fate that couldn't be overcome by scorn. The line was what passed for something terribly profound at the time. The most basic philosophical decision, according to Camus, was determining whether to live or to die in the face of the Absurd that is the state of the human condition. So I put the suicide question to myself.

As I looked at the pills and capsules, the mixture of colors, textures, and sizes, and played with them in my palm, it felt like a perverse head-game. I examined the tiny, printed number codes on the Dexamyls and the Dexedrines, the lettering on the Thorazines and Valiums.

"*There is always hope,*" I told myself. The possibility of things changing. Achieving what seemed like ever more elusive personal happiness. Manifesting more joy in my life, instead of relying on drugs as mood elevators and a means to get away from facing my problems.

I resolved a suicide solution: I would wait five years and revisit the question on that future birthday. See what my life looked like then.

It was an arbitrary choice, but it felt right.

COLORADO RIVER

Descending into the depths of the inner gorge below the Great Unconformity, I was running in the heart of the Grand Canyon. Five-thousand-foot-high Sumner Butte was like a lodestar on the other side of the Colorado, floating above me as I headed in its direction. The butte was named for John Sumner, a hunter and trapper with Major John Wesley Powell's first expedition into the Canyon in 1869, before Clarence Dutton attached his more fanciful spiritual monikers to formations higher up the North Rim.

The trail cut left and then right, curving its way along the walls of Vishnu Schist. For the most part, my pace was steady and fast. I wanted to take advantage of this last section of downhill running to make good time. I'd calculated that it was important to reach Phantom Ranch by the two-hour mark if I was to break six hours.

I arrived at a smooth area located on a promontory above the river. I'd stopped here to take in the view on my trial hike. To the west, the gorge opened up; the slim, pedestrian-only Silver Bridge was visible, spanning the river. Directly across the way from me was the low-lying area on the north bank where the SK went up to Phantom Ranch. Below and to my right was the Black Bridge for people, mules, and horses. Officially known as the Kaibab Suspension Bridge, the structure was five feet wide, 440 feet long, with 550-foot cables set into large reddish blocks that blended in with the surrounding rocks. During construction, the cables had to be unspooled and carried down the South Kaibab Trail by a team of 42 Havasupai tribesmen walking single file.

There had first been a rickety suspension bridge built by the park service, adjacent to where the Black Bridge was today. That initial span appeared in old Kolb brothers photos. It looked like something Indiana Jones might have encountered over a treacherous ravine in South America or some other part of the world, as he raced across with an adversary in hot pursuit, the bridge careening wildly from side to side.

The view east from the Black Bridge was obstructed by Vishnu Schist formations cascading into the river. Those formations had blocked access to the south side of the river when the National Park Service constructed the South Kaibab Trail in the mid-1920s. So the builders had blasted and bored a 30-foot tunnel through the mass of rock to connect the SK to the river and the Black Bridge.

Running past this viewpoint today, and just a couple hundred feet above the river, I encountered the wooden sign on a post that announced, "RIVER TRAIL," with an arrow pointing left. On the same sign were the words, "SOUTH KAIBAB," with an arrow pointing in the direction I was heading.

Before there was the Black Bridge, its unsteady wooden precursor, or the newer Silver Bridge, the River Trail was the main hiking route at the bottom of the Canyon. If you took the River Trail, you descended to the south bank of the Colorado where you continued west, parallel to the river, until you reached the hard left for the Bright Angel ascent. Now, few people used this portion of the River Trail, choosing instead to complete the journey down the South Kaibab through the tunnel and over the Black Bridge.

I continued running as the SK made a sharp, downward right turn. A steep drop on my left and some semi-submerged cross trail logs gave me pause, but I picked up speed anyway, anticipating the imminent crossing of the Colorado, which already felt like an exhilarating rite of passage.

Four young, dark-haired, shirtless guys came into view below, standing just outside the Black Bridge tunnel. They wore black Lycra running shorts, their hairless chests glistening in the sun. All of them looked to be in their early 20s, if that, with Latin complexions. They were smiling and laughing as they clowned around and posed for selfies.

Where had they come from?

At this point, I'd just assumed nobody else was ahead of me on the descent. Had they been in front of me the entire time? Jesus. But given what must have been a head start, along with their youth, it was no wonder they'd beaten me to the bottom.

Perhaps they were on their way *up* the South Kaibab?

The four of them disappeared from view, as the tunnel entrance was briefly out of sight, obscured by the rocky terrain around me. There were more of the cross-trail logs to negotiate, but I went faster anyway, still being careful to avoid a trip and fall. A final stone water break cut in front of me, and I cleared it.

For just a moment, I wished that I was running the Canyon thirty years earlier, in peak condition like when I was training for my first marathon during my short-lived return to running in the 1980s. I would be speeding down to the tunnel this morning, the wind blowing through the hair I still had back then. *Younger, vital, fleet of foot.*

I arrived at the tunnel entrance. The youths had vanished.

PART TWO

DOWN BY THE RIVER

CHAPTER 20

CROSSING THE BLACK BRIDGE

The Black Bridge tunnel entrance looked like an old mine, except for the mismatched stones arranged crudely around the rectangular opening for no apparent reason other than a decorative touch. I jogged inside. It was like entering a cave. There were no lights, and it quickly became darker within the rough-hewn walls. The only sound was my feet striking the dirt floor with muted thuds. As I approached the midway point of the tunnel, there was a bend, and for a moment, I could see neither the opening behind me nor the one up ahead. I was plunged into darkness.

#STUDENT REVOLUTIONARY: DENOUEMENT—1973

My suicide resolution was all well and good back in 1968. But sure enough, five years later did eventually roll around, along with my birthday, December 6, 1973. I recalled my decision from college. However, fate played a cruel trick on me. At 26, my life wasn't better. In fact, it was worse. I was living in a tiny, dilapidated $60-a-month room that had been converted from a garage behind a modest house in a marginal section of Oakland, California.

I was broke, unemployed, briefly collecting welfare and, for a time, food stamps. I'd left my girlfriend Honey behind on the East Coast a few months earlier. Now, I was spending my birthday alone, smoking some mediocre Mexican weed. My dinner was the same as it was virtually every night: a 23-cent McDonald's hamburger from down the street and a portion of brown rice from a large vat of the stuff I was cooking up weekly. To top off everything, I didn't have any wheels. I'd blown up the engine of my VW bus, operating it on too little oil due to a leak in the crankcase. As a result, I'd burnt a valve, which broke off and pierced the flat surface of its piston, the engine seizing up. I had the *Idiot's Guide*—officially, the oversized, spiral-bound volume titled, *How to Keep Your Volkswagon Alive: A Manual of Step-by-Step Procedures for the Compleat Idiot*—to instruct me in a rebuild. But first I needed some cash for parts.

On my birthday, after smoking the grass, I took out the pills from my stash. Preludins (chartreuse with chewy white-ish centers) were my current speed of choice. There were a few Valiums (the familiar pale-yellow 5 mgs and light-blue 10 mgs). A half-dozen Phenobarbitals (tiny white pills), a barbiturate. There were also some Dalmanes (green and black capsules), a part of the diazepam family and similar to Valium.

All of the pills in front of me were good in their own way if I wanted to blotto myself for a few hours, which I'd been doing pretty regularly. Or artificially raise my mood and energy with some speed. Or potentially, the Valiums, Phenobarbitals, and Dalmanes could be combined into a suicide solution.

Taking my own life was still a mind game, but I took my decision more seriously than five years earlier. In addition to my grim economic straits, I needed to find fresh meaning and direction in my life in the wake of the end of the anti-war movement and my own role as a committed political activist and sometime revolutionary: Chairman of Student Mobe at one of my college campuses; suspended for my part in SDS (Students for a Democratic Society) actions at another; cellmate of my hero, Chicago Seven defendant Abbie Hoffman, at the 1971 May Day mass civil disobedience protests in Washington, D.C.; and an "outside agitator" alongside Jerry Rubin, Hoffman's fellow Chicago Seven defendant, at another campus.

But when it came to consideration of suicide, I balked at the utter finality of it. Maybe there was some basic self-preservation instinct at work, something that kept me going. Some biological-psychological imperative. A will to live tied to a symbiotic operating system of body, mind, and spirit.

Whatever it was exactly, it pushed me forward. No matter how bad things seemed, I would get through it somehow. And if I could get through this, perhaps I could get through *anything*. More practically, while I was in that moment unemployed and broke, there was a temporary job I was waiting to hear about and would start soon if I got it: working on a crime survey for the U.S. Census Bureau, canvassing door-to-door in a sketchy section of Oakland—namely, the one I was living in. It was a job I could do on foot until I accumulated a few paychecks and went forward with that engine rebuild.

I put the pills back in their vial and placed the stash in its hiding place between the mattress on the floor and the wall.

There was still hope, I decided.

I burst out of the other end of the tunnel into bright sunshine. Immediately, I was running in glorious solitude across the Black Bridge, suspended 75 feet above the Colorado, nearly 5,000 feet below the South Rim, surrounded by the stark beauty of the inner gorge. There were cables above me, anchored into reddish concrete blocks on both sides of the river, supporting the bridge. Steel struts rose up next to me and connected to black railings with wire mesh for safety.

The bridge was wide enough for two people to pass each other from opposite directions, or for a mule, with some small space left on either side. Twin bolted-down planks ran the length of the span, protecting the cross-planking underneath from the pounding of the daily mule trains with their punishing hooves.

Halfway across on my left, I could see the sliver of the Silver Bridge in the distance, the flood plain before it with scattered boulders and patches of muted green. To my right, narrowing as it headed east, the gorge was composed of steep Vishnu Schist walls, a mixture of grays and browns with imbedded garnet nuggets that glowed crimson in the early morning light.

At the end of the bridge, where it met the north wall of the gorge, the trail cut sharply right and veered around and under the span. Once I was clear of the bridge, low rocks bordered the route as I trotted along the gently curving riverbank, the Colorado rushing by a few dozen yards away. Someone was splashing in the shallows near Boat Beach. I saw a couple kayaks on the sand. But a sign posted just off the trail offered a warning:

"COLORADO RIVER
Elevation 2,400
DANGEROUS CURRENT
Swimming Not Permitted
Purify Before Drinking."

On my trial hike, I'd gone down and stood where Boat Beach met the river. The water looked inviting. But you needed to think twice before venturing in, especially to swim—no matter how hot it was in the gorge. Among the *Death in Grand Canyon* stories were accounts of people who died in the Colorado: a river craft flipped, and passengers weren't wearing lifejackets; or a lifejacket was worn, but it caught on a branch, trapping a man underwater until he drowned. In 1992, two 16-year-old boys and a 22-year-old tried to swim across the river near the Black Bridge. The current swept them a mile downstream, where they became stuck in an eddy, and all three drowned as friends watched helplessly. In 1995, a man decided to swim the river—not across but stroking west from the Black Bridge. He died under Bright Angel Falls on the north bank, where the strong flowing creek entered the river. Also that year, an attempt by a 21-year-old male to swim across the river, further west at Pipe Creek, ended fatally. His body was recovered three weeks later, 19 miles downstream.

It wasn't just the current that was a danger. It was the freezing cold water released from the bottom of Lake Powell behind the Glen Canyon Dam to the east. Built in the 1960s to divert water south to Phoenix, the dam harnessed the Colorado, and generated electricity with its turbines. But it changed a variable-temperature river that once reflected the superheated summer air of the gorge and turned it instead into a year-round freezing flow.

By keeping the river so cold, the Glen Canyon Dam irrevocably altered the ecology of the Colorado. There was a loss of native fish as the warm waters of summer vanished. The dam also eliminated seasonal flashfloods that scoured the bottom of the gorge and flowed over the flood plain.

Man and nature co-exist at best, and all too often fail at even that.

Just ahead, the South Kaibab Trail split. I spotted the four young guys from the tunnel entrance taking the fork up to Phantom Ranch, moving smoothly and close together as they ran. I picked up my pace and felt the distance between us holding steady before they disappeared again around a bend. I couldn't expect to catch them. Thirty years earlier, when I was in top shape, it would have been a different story—so long as I chased them down in smarter fashion than I ran my first marathon back then.

MARATHON FIASCO

Almost 20 years to the day after my suicide resolution in that abysmal Oakland converted garage, I was living in Los Angeles. My digs still weren't great—a one-bedroom basement apartment in a funky part of Hollywood—but I'd worked my way up from a TV station news production assistant job to associate producing and then producing local programming: talk shows, live specials, segments for a magazine show, and an Emmy-nominated documentary. Next, I took a network Broadcast Standards censor job, of all things, at ABC—with a plan to only do it for a year and then move on to a different network position or go back to a television station in a more senior capacity.

I was soon frustrated by my responsibilities enforcing the network's arcane rules when it came to content permitted on shows like *Laverne & Shirley*, *Mork & Mindy*, *General Hospital*, *Hollywood Squares*, and *American Bandstand*. Whether it was informing *General Hospital* that ABC rules prohibited star Tony Geary from uttering the word "horny," or placing sexual-innuendo limits on *Hollywood Squares*, or needing to tell the sitcom *Making a Living* to cut back on how many times they said "pregnant." And on *American Bandstand*, trying to figure out what LA. punk band X was *really* singing in the lyrics to "Motel Room in My Bed." Were they sneaking in a "fucking"? Plus, there was my failure to hit my one-year exit strategy.

I returned to running for the first time since lettering in cross-country my freshman year of college. Running became an outlet for my job discontent, and a way to find meaningful accomplishment elsewhere: racing and hitting target times. Before long, I was trained up for the 1983 Western Hemisphere Marathon and its 26.2 mile course. I went from running 40 miles a week to 50, then 60, even 70. Breaking four hours was my goal. Maybe more like 3:30.

Race day dawned in Culver City, not far from Century City where I was working at ABC. It was sunny, with a crowded field of runners. Soon, I was racing alongside a tall, lanky, younger guy. We introduced ourselves. His name was Robert.

"Looks like we're doing about the same pace," I said.

"Yeah, I just want to keep cranking out eight-minute miles."

"Me too."

"How many marathons have you done?"

"First one," I said.

Runners were strung out behind and in front of us along Jefferson Boulevard on the way to Playa Del Rey and the ocean, where there was the turnaround back to Culver City.

My running partner stopped for water, but I felt fine. I wasn't thirsty. So I skipped the water breaks and snacks as he tanked up on both. After each pause, I slowed a bit to wait for him, and he would then catch up.

We cranked out more eight-minute miles under a sun that was quickly becoming warmer. As we hit the five, seven, and 10-mile markers we passed people who'd gone out too fast. Volunteers called out mile times, and I checked my watch.

We reached 10 miles in an hour and 20 minutes, an even eight minutes a mile; double that and 20 would be in 2:40 with six miles to go. If I picked up speed around Mile 15 or 16, and especially for the final 6.2 miles, breaking three and a half hours was a possibility.

But by Mile 12, I wasn't feeling so good. By Mile 14, I said, "I gotta take a walking break."

"Really? Are you sure?" Robert said.

"Yeah."

"I can slow down just a bit."

"No, it's okay. Go for it."

Robert went on ahead as I walked and was passed by the same people I'd passed earlier. I started running again after a few minutes, only to need to walk some more. From there, I ran in fits and starts.

By Mile 19, I hit the wall. I was in agony. The day was hot now as I walked those last few brutal miles back into Culver City. Finally, with the end of the race in sight, I started to run and staggered across the finish line. I wasn't close to finishing in three and a half hours. In fact, I didn't even break four. My time was 4:03:49.

I grabbed the available orange wedges, cookies, some water, and Gatorade, and started stuffing my face. Almost immediately, I began to feel better, and I got a bloody blistered toe fixed up at the medical tent.

The next day, I went back to my running books and took a closer look. My biggest mistake jumped out at me immediately: You were supposed to start drinking water *before* you felt thirsty in a marathon. And I didn't know about electrolytes—chemicals the body needs to have replenished for long runs. I didn't eat anything beforehand. Or during the race. I should have consumed some edible gels, power bars, or Gatorade as I ran. Even cookies and candy bars in a pinch.

Lesson learned.

I stayed with running through the following year, before quitting for another decade, done in by driving myself relentlessly, overtraining to the point of creating physical problems, including ongoing endless fatigue, the joy of running gone.

CHAPTER 21

PHANTOM RANCH

THIS WAS THEIR LAND

Running alongside the Colorado River on the SK, I reached wooden signs where the young guys had disappeared: "PHANTOM RANCH" and "NORTH KAIBAB TRAIL," with an arrow pointing up ahead and to the right. Also "BRIGHT ANGEL TRAIL" with an arrow pointing left.

Here where the trail split was a double-sided Canyon history display, sheltered under a small, overhanging pitched roof. The roof was just big enough to provide some shade from the relentless sun for anyone examining the panels presenting photographs and history of the Bright Angel Trail—prospectors, adventurers, and fortune seekers on horses, and images of tribal hieroglyphs. Back at Boat Beach, there was a separate display devoted to Native Americans that focused on pueblo ruins on the other side of the river.

This had once been their land: the Havasupai, Hopi, Paiute, and Navajo. They fished the untamed Colorado that was their lifeblood and the center of their myths. They hunted game: rabbit, deer, and elk. The Havasupai created the original Bright Angel Trail to facilitate their seasonal occupation of Indian Garden, where they maintained the irrigation systems they had built there, utilizing the year-round water of Garden Creek running through it. In the spring and summer months, they grew small crops of corn, squash, and beans. In the fall and winter, the upper Canyon had snow, turning the trail treacherous and making farming impossible, so the tribe lived up on the Kaibab Plateau as hunter-gatherers.

In the Paiute language, Kaibab means "mountain lying down;" it was their name for the Grand Canyon. According to Paiute legend, the god Taavotz created the Colorado River and warned that anyone who tried to follow it west would be swallowed up. One can imagine their surprise when adventurer John Wesley Powell and his small flotilla showed up August 15, 1869, arriving on the river from the east and heading west, exploring and mapping the Canyon. Powell was taken with the beauty of this spot where I was now, amid the semi-arid Canyon. He named the nearby clear rushing stream Bright Angel Creek.

Before becoming Phantom Ranch, the location was known as Rust's Camp, after the former teacher David Rust who first developed it into a hunting and tourist stopover with some tents in the early 1900s. Visitors had initially been ferried across the river. Then, in 1907, Rust built a contraption on a pulley system that was known as the "cable tram"—a cage big enough to hold one mule or several people. An old Kolb brothers photo, circa 1908, shows three people on benches inside the cage, two of them women attired in western hats, blouses, and skirts. The rickety suspension bridge replaced the cable tram in 1921, followed by the Black Bridge.

In 1903, President Theodore Roosevelt made that first visit to the Canyon in the wake of Buckey O'Neill's death in Cuba, descending the Bright Angel and staying at Rust's Camp to hunt mountain lions on the North Rim. On his way down the Bright Angel, Roosevelt encountered Havasupai—several families who were farming Indian Garden. Through an interpreter, Roosevelt told the Havasupai they would need to leave, because the area was being turned into a national park, which as noted Congress declared in 1919. Eventually, in 1928, the last of the Havasupai were pushed out by the National Park Service in a forced relocation to a reservation at the west end of the Canyon.

On my trial hike, I'd paused to review the display and consider its implications. The book *Bury My Heart at Wounded Knee* had changed everything when it came out in the early 1970s. It was part of the consciousness raising of the times, creating a visceral awareness of the Native American genocide.

A few people were scattered about the trail fork exhibit today as I ran past it; they were making their way after breaking camp. I took the turn right at the trail junction. Bright Angel Creek rushed by on my left, completing its journey from the North Rim to the Colorado. As I moved along the gentle incline, it felt good to change to running uphill. I fancied myself a stronger-than-average hill runner. One of my half-marathons was the 1999 Forest of Nisene Marks in Santa Cruz. It offered a relentless, Redwood-forested ridge climb and fast downhill trails that required jumping logs—a hazard that resulted in a runner near me taking a wicked fall then getting up bloodied and continuing on their way. I'd been pleased to come in a few minutes under two hours in that race, hauling ass like all get-out on the final mile to break that barrier, finishing in 1:56:36.

As I ran up Phantom Ranch, the trail was light brown earth with rows of guide stones. Overall, the running was smooth. I went past a smattering of cottonwood trees as I headed up into a box canyon surrounded by rocky cliffs.

A mule deer wandered in front of me only a couple dozen yards away and grazed along the trail. The creature lifted its head and gave me an unafraid stare as I approached; its namesake ears twitched.

"Well, aren't you the fearless one?" I said, as I kept running, closer now.

The animal lowered its head and returned to chewing brush and grass, the bulk of its body blocking my way. It was shorter, stockier, and less graceful than the whitetail deer I grew up with as a young child in New Jersey. I would creep up on a small herd of the animals in the field down the street from our suburban house, seeing how close I could get to them undetected from downwind, before they would scatter into the woods with their bounding leaps, their tails in upright warning.

I slowed down and was only a few feet away when the mule deer finally ambled off the trail, and I trotted by. It was a cool man-and-nature-in-harmony moment, but disconcerting. The deer's fearlessness wasn't the natural order of things.

There was no hunting permitted in Grand Canyon National Park. The gray wolf—the primary natural predator of mule deer—hadn't been seen in the Canyon since wolves were hunted to extinction in the 1940s to protect area livestock. Mountain lions, another predator, had become rare, with only few radio-collared animals on the North Rim.

With nothing to fear, small herds of deer freely wandered the South Rim. There were even solo majestic elk, or sometimes a male and female with a calf or two in tow. At dusk and in the early morning hours, the deer boldly headed down the roads around the Grand Canyon Village, sometimes not even bothering to scatter for approaching cars. Rather, the vehicles had to make way for the creatures, as children and their parents thrilled at their proximity to "wild" animals, snapping photos as the kids squealed with delight.

THE STORY OF ECHO

In October of 2014, an unidentified visitor to the Canyon would take a photo of a wolf standing by the side of the road, up on the North Rim. The animal faced the camera, looking much like a wayward, oversized German Shepherd, and was poised as if patiently waiting to cross the pavement until the visitor's car moved on. The wolf was the first of its kind to be seen at the Canyon in over 60 years.

The photo went viral and caused an internet sensation. Known to researchers as 914F, the three-year-old female had been radio-collared nine months earlier near Cody, Wyoming. Re-introduced from Canadian packs in the 1990s, wolves were flourishing in western Wyoming. The collar had since become inoperable, and wildlife officials hoped to outfit her with a new one. Meanwhile, school children around the world entered an online contest to name the wolf. A 10-year-old boy in Oregon won with his choice, Echo. Echo had left the Rocky Mountains of southwestern Wyoming, going south, searching for a mate and fresh territory to start a pack. As was the case in the Grand Canyon, wolves in Utah had been exterminated decades ago as a livestock threat, but they were now protected from hunting by the Endangered Species Act.

Echo passed through northern Utah with its wooded canyons, plateaus and gorges, dodging detection by humans. She continued south past the still-visible waterlines of what was once giant, prehistoric Lake Bonneville. She bypassed Salt Lake City and went nearly 250 miles further, all the way to the red sandstone desert formations of Monument Valley, where she crossed into Arizona, reached the Grand Canyon, and was photographed.

Before officials could attempt to fit Echo with a new radio collar, she was on the move again. Unable to find a mate in the wolfless Canyon, Echo headed back north, retracing her steps into Utah. Two months after being sighted at the Canyon, Echo was shot and killed by a hunter, 155 miles south of Provo. The hunter said he observed an injured steer in a ranch field and saw something in the brush nearby that he thought was a coyote—legal to shoot in Utah and carrying a $50 bounty. He pulled the trigger, ending Echo's remarkable odyssey.

Using DNA testing of scat samples taken at the Canyon, the U.S. Fish and Wildlife Service confirmed the three-year-old animal was Echo, still wearing her radio collar. An autopsy found elk and deer fur in her stomach from hunting, but no livestock. She weighed a healthy 89 pounds at the time of her death, having successfully foraged her way north.

Echo had travelled an estimated 750 miles in her quest to find a mate.

"It is nothing short of a tragedy that this wolf's journey across the west was cut short," Eva Sargent, a director for Defenders of Wildlife, told a local newspaper. "This brave and ambitious female gray wolf . . . had already become a symbol of what gray wolf recovery should look like: animals naturally dispersing to find suitable habitat."

"It's very sad news," added Michael Robinson, a conservationist at the Center for Biological Diversity. "We and a lot of other people were rooting for her. Echo's death illustrates the peril wolves face even under the protection of the Endangered Species Act." The act provides a penalty of up to a year in prison and a $50,000 fine for crimes involving an endangered species. The hunter turned himself in and wasn't prosecuted.

In addition to the famous photograph of Echo waiting by the side of the road, there was another picture of her taken on the North Rim. Echo sits in the grass and brush at dusk against a backdrop of slender pines, her head thrown back, her radio collar visible, as she howls for a mate—and awaits a response that never came.

Running up through Phantom Ranch, I arrived at the upper footbridge across Bright Angel Creek. The wooden bridge led to 32 permit-only camping sites in a strip of land up against the box canyon's western wall. It was a popular location that generally needed to be booked well in advance. I jogged across the bridge, with its cross-planks and the spaces between, the stream visible below, rushing past. Off to the right, on the other side of the bridge, stood an oversized, oval temperature gauge mounted on a post. It read a still-comfortable 70 degrees—a long way from the 100-plus it would reach later in the day.

People were up and around near their tents, some preparing breakfast, several exploring the creek, others getting ready to break camp for the tough hike out. I trotted back across the bridge and turned left. The Phantom Ranch Ranger Station was visible off to the right, an American flag listless on its pole. Another fork in the trail soon greeted me. One branch went along Bright Angel Creek, but I took the other and passed a sign positioned overhead on my left: "WELCOME TO PHANTOM RANCH." There was a corral with mules inside, a couple guys in cowboy gear tending to them.

Two hikers—a young guy and a girl—walked toward me. Each carried a large backpack with a sleeping bag rolled underneath, and they used hiking poles. They reminded me of the young pair I'd met on the shuttle to the SK trailhead.

"Hi. Either of you know the time?"

"Sure," the guy replied, glancing at his wrist. "6:45."

I'd made it to Phantom Ranch in two hours flat and was on pace to break six.

"Thanks." I took off again.

I was startled by the four young guys suddenly upon me and moving at a fast pace. I eased over to give them room to pass. Their youthfulness was even more striking up close. Their leader was handsome and carried himself with an easy grace in black running tights, a purple refillable water bottle attached at his waist and a running watch on his wrist. The others were close behind. One had on an Arizona State University cap, and another one, who was noticeably taller than the rest, carried a small daypack hung around his hip. Only the last one—separating just a bit from the rest and lagging a few yards behind—seemed to notice me with a glance.

I got back on the trail and headed past a number of cabins all built with same motif: walls constructed of rough stone; a rock chimney rising from each rustic, sloped, teal-green roof with overhanging eaves; and windows that were green-trimmed with old-style small glass panes. The little Phantom Ranch cantina and store came into view and replicated the look of the visitor cabins.

It was a woman, Mary Jane Colter, who designed the distinctive stone and green wood-trimmed buildings in 1922. Colter was a rarity for her time: a female architect. In addition to Phantom Ranch, she designed the Bright Angel Lodge, did work decorating the El Tovar Hotel with its log cabin-meets-opulent-hunting-lodge motif, and created an imposing stone house built in 1914 at Hermit's Rest on the South Rim. As always with Colter's work, everything was constructed from local materials that blended in with the environment. Colter is also credited with naming Phantom Ranch—for Phantom Creek, a tributary of Bright Angel Creek.

I pulled up out front of the cantina and store. It didn't open until later, but there was nothing I needed. On my hike, I'd visited its interior. There was the store in front, and it opened up to the eating area, which featured several long wooden tables with chairs for breakfast and dinner service to campers who signed up in advance. A blackboard listed the store goods in white chalk: beverages, from lemonade to tea and even wine; snacks, including peanut butter, bagels, and some fruit; sandwiches that needed to be pre-ordered; hiking aids, such as refillable water bottles and purification pellets; headlamps, if you realized you were going to be hiking back up in the dark; sunscreen, ponchos, and souvenirs—shirts, hats, bandanas, and patches. You could even buy a postcard and a stamp and have it mailed and marked as from Phantom Ranch via mule train. There was also an informative posting of sunrise and sunset times, as well as the day's weather and anticipated temperatures.

The cantina and the area outside served as a gathering place for the overnighting campers as well as those hiking the Canyon. A spigot was mounted out front for refilling water bottles. It all made for a nice break under the trees during a hike—"nice" depending at least partly on the temperature. There were several large boulders you could sit on, along with a couple picnic tables where a few hikers sat, gear at their feet.

There was a bathroom off to the right, but I ignored it and walked around to the creek side of the store where I found a tree and put down my daypack. After relieving myself, I quick-changed, taking off my Coolibar T-Shirt. Then, I peeled off my long-sleeved Asics stretch-top, which I placed in the daypack before I put on the T-shirt again. I hustled through my actions, not wanting to spend more than a few minutes on my break. I debated eating one of the peanut-butter-and-honey sandwiches, but I was still feeling full from my feast the night before.

I hoisted my daypack and, carrying the partially full bottle of water in my hand, set out at an easy jog. I could see two guys in front of the store at a picnic table, getting their gear together, and another one filling several containers at the spigot. The Trans-Canyon Pipeline was obviously working here. There only remained the break at the bottom of Bright Angel Trail. I didn't know if I'd find a crew working to fix it, the flow of water up Bright Angel disrupted, or if the repair had already been completed. Given I still had four full water bottles, I wasn't concerned either way.

I continued to run, retracing my steps down the gentle incline, past the mule corral, the ranger station, and the upper Bright Angel footbridge. Reaching the trail fork at the double-sided Canyon history display, I turned right, and headed west. I crossed the lower Bright Angel Creek footbridge and then came the old National Park Service mule corral with its one-story stone buildings—wooden roofs intact, but projecting disarray and disuse, with wheelbarrows and tools strewn about, suggesting a restoration in progress. I saw the young couple that had given me the time and passed them with a wave as the guy called out, "Have a good one!"

Proceeding along the trail, I emerged from a scattering of trees. Up ahead, the Silver Bridge floated across the Colorado, straddling the river with elegant simplicity. There was a mild bow to the slender span, rising up from each side to its center. A spindly tower on the north bank stood perhaps 30 feet high, a suspension cable sloping down and then curving back up to another tower that was set almost up against the south wall of the gorge. The towers were comprised of steel framing, which appeared delicate, like the bridge itself, all thin graceful lines and lightweight suspension.

Completed in 1970, the Silver Bridge carried the Trans-Canyon Pipeline underneath it and immediately became the primary way to access the Bright Angel Trail from Phantom Ranch. Previously, that required doubling back along the river to the Black Bridge and traversing what was now the largely ignored eastern stretch of the River Trail.

I crossed the Silver Bridge at an easy pace. Restricted to people, with no mules or horses allowed, it was so narrow that you had to turn sideways to permit someone else to pass. The metal grate walkway made a "thunk-thunk-thunk" sound beneath my feet. I peered down through the steel latticework with its parallel lengthwise slots. I could see the Trans-Canyon Pipeline—black, cylindrical, and held in place by braces, slung maybe a foot below the walkway and directly under the middle of the span.

As with the Black Bridge, wire safety mesh came up to chest level along the railings on both sides. Looking to the east, I could see the Vishnu Schist cliffs and the narrow flood plain on the south side of the river. The Black Bridge was visible about a mile away with mountains of rock beyond it, as the gorge narrowed. To the west, the base of the North Rim slope spilled into the river. The flood plain continued on the south side, partly covered in boulders along with low, sparse vegetation. In the distance, the two sides of the gorge drew together, as the river disappeared between them before it turned to the southwest and exited the Canyon nearly 100 miles away.

The Silver Bridge

CHAPTER 22

RIVER TRAIL TRAGEDY

I finished running across the Silver Bridge to where it T-boned into the River Trail. If you turned left here and followed the River Trail, it connected with the SK below the Great Arc at the trail junction I'd passed on my descent. I cut right and headed west, past the wooden sign on a post: "BRIGHT ANGEL TRAIL," with an arrow pointing in that direction. The Trans-Canyon Pipeline also continued its journey, as it dropped down just above the old flood plain and paralleled the river above ground.

As I ran, the trail rose up quickly, looping along the south wall of the gorge, scaling its heights. On my practice hike, I'd thought, "Good. Let's get the ascent started!" After all, I still had nine miles and 4,700 feet of elevation gain to go. Within a few minutes, I was about 100 feet above the river. I'd rounded a bend, only to discover the route immediately plunged down to the river. I was back to square one. On top of that, I'd soon encountered a stretch that was like trying to slog through soft beach sand. Today, as I ran, that same stretch sucked the effort out of me, especially with the weight of the daypack and its bottled waters. I decided to briefly walk.

There's a romantic notion about running on a beach. In reality, that's only truly practical at the shoreline, when the sand is left flat and hard by the retreating tide. Running on Los Angeles-area beaches never held a lot of appeal for me, and besides they were an hour drive from Studio City. But it was a whole other story on summer family vacations in Maine with Kathy and the girls, where beaches were right out the front door, scenic and broken up by rocky wilderness coastline.

I especially liked to run early mornings from our Kennebunkport rental that faced the ocean, heading out along Sea Road as it cut inland to Four Corners, where I would turn west on Route 9, past woods and scattered houses. Crossing the Mousam River, I ran by the fisherman stationed on the bridge with their poles, hoping to catch sea bass that swam upstream with the tide. Then, I'd cut left down a country lane, going past a farm with horses in a field, arriving where the road met the sand dunes of Parson's Beach and a path that led to the ocean.

With a high-stepping motion, I tried to keep the sand out of my shoes and make it to the hard, darker, tide-flattened sand by the water's edge. There, I sped up, the sea sparkling on my left, the sun reflecting off the waves. Just me, the Atlantic, the sun and the sky, virtually no one else around, if it was early enough in the day; the beach my own joy-of-running-paradise.

While in Kennebunkport, we participated as a family in the annual July 4th Day at the Beach celebration. It was a festive affair: At nightfall, everyone gathered at the ocean's edge, armed with blankets and foldable chairs to watch the fireworks. Sparklers kept the girls and their cousins occupied before the main event, which was staged on an empty, nearby rocky spit of land across from the huge rambling bulk of the Narragansett—a one-time turn-of-the-century hotel, now converted to condos, although with its distinctive wood-shingled exterior left unchanged.

The kids were younger then, my role as a father more defined. As the fireworks exploded in the night sky to the oohs and ahs of everyone around me—following the delights of the lobster feast we had all shared beforehand—I was overwhelmed by a sense of family and tradition that I'd never expected to experience in the wake of those earlier, seemingly irrevocable choices that I'd made in my younger days.

#STUDENT REVOLUTIONARY: ON THE ROAD—KENNEBUNKPORT, MAINE

My first time in Kennebunkport I was in a hearse. It was July 1971, a couple months after I was in jail with Abbie Hoffman. I'd been living alone in a Hell's Kitchen fifth-floor walk-up in Manhattan. There was no air conditioning in my squalid one-room tenement during a summer heat wave. Just me, sweltering along with the cockroaches, the endless ants, and a rat that came out from under the kitchen sink at night.

A friend of mine from college showed up in a black Cadillac hearse he'd purchased used from a funeral parlor. After picking up his girlfriend, we hit the road and drove through New England and on to Canada. We camped out, got stoned, and were regularly pulled over by the cops. My stash survived their searches undetected, secure in a little tool compartment I'd discovered next to one of the chrome casket rollers in the hearse's coffin bay. The hiding place was shielded from police detection by the old mattress we'd tossed inside and where we slept up against each other, waking in the morning as a jumble of legs, arms, and feet.

Driving up the Maine coast, we detoured from Route 1 to head through quaint Kennebunkport with its T-shirt stores, boutiques, and restaurants. We received plenty of stares, but no police harassment. I had a favorable first impression of the small, scenic resort town bustling in the middle of summer tourist season. But if you'd told me then that, 26 years later, I was going to return as a husband and a father with Kathy and our toddler, celebrating Cassidy's first birthday with a Winnie the Pooh cake, followed by another dozen years of annual Kennebunkport family vacations, it would have been inconceivable to me.

Today in the Canyon, the soft sandy stretch of the River Trail gave way to dirt, and I went back to running. I came around a curve and was surprised to see one of the four young guys leaning up against a rock, shirtless and sweating. I recognized him as the last of the four—the one who'd lagged behind.

"Are you okay?" I asked, pausing.

"Yeah, just tired."

"Do you have enough water? I've got extra."

"Nah, thanks. I'm good," he said, and he shook the container in his hand. "It's still mostly full. And it's not really too hot out yet."

"Where are your pals?"

"They decided to go on ahead. We're supposed to meet up at Indian Garden."

"So, you guys are doing the SK up Bright Angel loop?"

"We were actually gonna to do rim-to-rim and get picked up by my mom, but we found out about the North Kaibab Trail washout and had to change our plans."

"Right, right. By the way, I wondered how you guys got so far ahead of me on the descent. Were you on that first hiker's bus?"

"Yeah."

"I was right behind you on the shuttle. You must have been really moving on the way down."

"Yep. We had clear sailing."

"You guys travel light. Not even a fanny pack," I said, indicating his bare hip, only a black T-shirt tied around it.

"Bernardo has the daypack—power bars."

"Got it. Well, I should get going."

"See you up ahead, maybe," he said.

"Okay." I started to run at a good pace to make up for stopping. I was pleased to have caught up to one of them. Somewhere up ahead, the other three were running.

I was surprised at their lack of planning. Rim-to-rim with only a small daypack and power bars? That route was 24 miles instead of the SK Bright Angel loop's 17, and he was clearly having his fill even with the shorter version.

I ran up another incline. The Vishnu cliffs dropped straight down to the river here. In the 1880s, geologist Charles Walcott had named the rocks after the Vishnu Temple on the North Rim where, on one side of the otherwise flat top of an eroded, giant butte, there arose a pyramid-like rock formation. The Vishnu Temple moniker had been bestowed by fellow geologist Clarence Dutton a few years before.

Mountains once stood here, eroded over hundreds of millions of years. The Vishnu Schist was the core of those mountains, which had been formed by the collision of tectonic plates. Two billion years ago, the Schist had its beginnings as layers of sedimentary silt and mud that were a part of a river, lake, or an inland sea. The mud and silt had been subjected to heat and pressure over millions of years, transforming sedimentary layers into the hardened schist. This occurred somewhere on the northwest portion of the planet's first known supercontinent, Columbia. Also known as Nuna or Hudsonland, Columbia was the supercontinent before Pangaea, Pannotia, and Rodinia—its existence only recently confirmed by scientists in the early 2000s.

Columbia was estimated to have been about 8,000 miles long and 4,000 miles wide—about a third the size of all the land on Earth today, with much remaining to be created over hundreds of millions of years by volcanism, uplift, and erosion. As with Rodinia, there was no life on land yet. There were only single-cell primal organisms in the ocean.

The Vishnu rocks that formed at the time of Columbia should be buried deep inside the Earth, but were exposed all around me, the Grand Canyon a portal to the planet's past incarnations. As was the case when I traversed the remnants of Pangaea, I was now running on what was once a supercontinent, but this one *from two billion years ago.*

After another upward trail feint, I was back at almost river-level, running alongside the old flood plain. Some people in a pair of kayaks passed by me on the Colorado. I saw a few bright tents along the shore; somebody was cooking breakfast on a Coleman stove. I checked behind me but didn't see the young guy catching up.

Columbia began to break up about 1.6 billion years ago. The land masses rode off on their tectonic plates, pulled apart in slow motion, splintering a few inches a year in different directions in the ongoing planetary cycle of birth, death, and rebirth.

DEATH IN THE FAMILY

My return to Kennebunkport should have been a couple years earlier than the first trip Kathy and I made with Cassidy in 1997. But fate had intervened and almost destroyed a family. In the process, I learned that the greatest risk you can take in life is to create a life—in this case, Josh, an infant born prematurely three years before Cassidy.

Memories: NICU, isolettes, emotional exhaustion. So much time with staff—the doctors and nurses and orderlies. We saw them more than any friends we had. And sometimes, they felt more important than any friends.

The alternating desperation and hope. Taking Josh home from the hospital after a couple months was itself a miracle. We only had him home at all because Kathy, using every bit of her RN skills, could oversee his daily onslaught of medications and breathing treatments. I did what I could to assist.

Kathy sang softly to Josh while in the hospital and later at home. She memorialized everything in an album with lift-up clear pages that she devoted to him. There was another album filled with his photos. At the end of it she wrote down the words to her lullaby:

"Mommy loves you, Daddy loves you
Daddy loves you, Mommy loves you
Sleep well little baby boy
Bye-lo, Bye-lo little baby boy"

She transcribed the ongoing dialogue she had with him cradled in her arms and looking up at her:

"Who's that boy? Who's that
special, precious boy? So-o-o
special, Mommy's boy, Mommy's
loving you. So special boy. So
special, precious boy. Who's that
special boy? Mommy's seeing you.
She sees those beautiful eyes
and eyelashes, those special ears.
Mommy sees those special toes.
Special boy, Mommy's so special
Boy . . ."

There was a uterine fibroid that had shortened his allotted time in the womb, a matter of as little as ten more days, or a full couple of weeks lost that could have placed him at the tipping point in favor of survival.

As his face and body became chubbier from steroid treatments for his underdeveloped lungs, there was still the hope against hope he would somehow make it, no matter how much the doctors cautioned. There were his bright eyes with their connection to the people around him, his laughter as he played with the mobile hung over his bed, his intense focus on the bright yellow of the *Sesame Street* Big Bird plush toy in his crib.

There was the emotional shredding. Questioning everything when you weren't so deep under water in the thick of it that you couldn't think straight. The desperate desire for everything to just be normal and to work out somehow.

A first Father's Day card, written in big flowery script by a nurse we had grown close to, was on a square of paper:

"Hi DAD!
I love you! You are the
Best-est Dad and I'm
Sending you big hugs & kisses
HAPPY FIRST DAD'S DAY
Josh"

There was a heart on the "i" in "Hi" and another at the bottom, along with x's and o's and "his" signature.

How could one go from parent to childless without a mental collapse? Your infant is in crisis as you try not to think the unthinkable. Process what the doctors are telling you. The updates, the updates, always the updates. Then, to have your child ripped away from you . . .

A photo the morning he died: a close-up of him back in the hospital, intubated, eyes closed, the feeding tube to his stomach, his Big Bird beside him. Another photo: Kathy and I crying, heads bent over Josh. A final photo of the two of us holding hands over him with a caption by Kathy:

"November 27, 1994
Mom and Dad hold Josh for
the last time. Peacefully, he died
as we spoke to him:
Goodbye Special precious boy
Mommy and Daddy are loving you
You are not alone
We will miss you, but you will not
Be forgotten
Our special special boy"

Death: the nadir of an emotional hell that had consumed us for months. You suffer through the blackest time, together, as only the two of you can. You try to hold on and keep it together and move forward.

The cremation of our eight-month-old baby boy in a tiny coffin-like container, the both of us there to witness it and then take him home again. The grey granite urn with his ashes that we carried with us, and that Kathy placed next to her side of our bed.

You stage a celebration of a life and invite friends and relatives. Photos of Josh, a favorite one of him wearing a blue-and-yellow onesie and happy in his bouncy chair, smiling.

Then, you live for a very long time in a fog after the months of effort, tension, hope, fear, and in the end, despair. The house around you now desolate.

There was a touching note Kathy wrote on a small piece of paper near the end of the memories album:

"A small sadness:
Josh was teething for the first time
at the time of his death. His bottom
front teeth almost made it through."

I forged ahead on the River Trail, almost level with the flood plain. The route rose up again to where there was another stretch of loose sand. I persevered running it this time, my shoes having a problem with their grip and making a "squish-squish-squish" sound. Willpower was driving me—a must-do determination to climb out of the depths of the Canyon.

PART THREE

THE ASCENT

CHAPTER 23

PIPE CREEK RAVINE

Pipe Creek was abruptly in front of me. There was the sharp left turn onto Bright Angel Trail that wasn't marked with a sign that I could see, despite its importance. On my trial hike, I had stopped here and looked around. I hadn't yet purchased the detailed trail map of the Canyon that I carried with me this time. The greenery at the stream—the trees, bushes, and grasses—had added to my confusion as I wondered "if this was where I'm supposed to be?"

Today, I made the turn without hesitation and continued running. I was in a ravine a few dozen yards across. The trail paralleled Pipe Creek, the running surface relatively smooth up an incline. I jogged past the River Rest House—a small structure offering no water, just pit toilets and an emergency phone. I wasn't sure exactly where the Trans-Canyon Pipeline break was, but for some reason, I'd pictured it here. There were no signs of work crews, so as far as I knew, everything was in order for water refills on the way up.

I still was only two-thirds through my first bottled water. Four full ones remained in my daypack. I was ready for anything. If the pump house at Indian Garden decided to stop working this very instant, I would be glad I'd lugged the extra water with me.

The walls grew higher, the ravine broadening as I ascended alongside Pipe Creek, which was only a few inches deep at this time of year and pooling in places. It was another story when the rains came. I knew the creek became a raging torrent during storms, roaring down the ravine like the flashfloods detailed in *Death in Grand Canyon*. All seemed calm today, but I could see how you might need to scurry uphill to safety at other times.

The trail moved back and forth, switching sides in the ravine, crisscrossing the stream on rows of rocks lined up in the water. I danced carefully across the first row that I encountered, not wanting to slip and subject my feet to the grueling climb up ahead in soggy shoes and socks—although at least I had that backup pair of socks in my daypack.

There came the sound of pounding feet behind me. I turned to look. It was a guy who was maybe in his late 20s and close to six feet tall with wild blondish hair. His full backpack looming over his head made him appear even taller. He was moving along at a wicked-fast hiking pace, overtaking me.

I moved to make room for him.

"You're hiking faster than I'm running," I said as he caught me. "Mind if I join you?"

"Suit yourself, dude," he said as he passed me.

I fell into place, jogging off his right shoulder and picking up speed to keep up.

"You're motoring," I said. "Guess it's good to get out of here before it's 105."

"Fuck that shit," he said, without turning to look at me. "It was 113 in the gorge yesterday. Going to hit that again today. Just give it a few hours."

"Were you at Bright Angel Campground?"

"Yep."

We reached a water crossing. He went over the row of rocks without hesitation, skipping every other stone. I went across more slowly, balancing myself carefully on the top of each one. I had to run faster on the other side to catch up.

"So how did you deal with the heat?"

"Lots of people got in the creek during the afternoon, me included. Wading and just sitting in the water—letting it wash over you."

"Sounds nice."

"Yep. Stayed brutal until pretty late. I did some 4-2-0, a brewski, and got lit. The stars were like diamonds."

"Yeah, quite the challenge to stay cool, I imagine," I said.

"That was nothing. The challenge was getting there. There was a trail washout on the North Kaibab."

"I heard about that. So, you were coming down from the North Rim?"

"Yep."

"Wasn't the trail closed?"

"Yeah, technically. Total bullshit. Got there before they could post a ranger. The trail got dangerous as shit at the washout. Almost lost my pack, not to mention myself. There was about 45 feet of trail gone. *Just fucking gone.* Goddamn Trans-Canyon Pipeline—piece of shit. If you want a real pipeline, don't build it outta fucking aluminum. Steel pipe is the way to go."

We crossed the stream on another row of rocks—these of markedly differing sizes. He skipped hitting all of the rocks again and was across quickly, moving up the trail. I landed on each rock and had to again speed up to catch him.

"Come to the Canyon a lot?"

"Most every year. My girlfriend drove me to the North Rim. I tried to get her to join me, but she begged off. She knew I didn't plan to do this in slow motion. When you're in, you're all in, and then, when it's time to get out, you get out—fast."

The ravine around us was getting wider.

"So you're doing rim-to-river and back up?" he said.

"Yeah."

"First time?"

"Well, I hiked it a few weeks ago. This time, I'm running it. Well, almost all of it. Going to have to power-hike some of it up ahead. I'm trying to break six hours."

"Rad! Stick with me." He turned and looked back at me. "How old are you anyway, dude?"

I hesitated. "Sixty-four."

"*No shit!*" He glanced back again. "Six hours is good, especially considering—"

"My decrepitude?"

"Well, I'm about to hit the big 3-0 myself. Hope I'm still doing this, you know—"

"At my age?"

"Sorry, dude." He kept pounding along like a man on a mission, me jogging off his shoulder. He may not have had a time goal, but he seemed more driven than I was. I wondered how long I could keep up with him. On a good day, it shouldn't have been too much of a problem, but I was beginning to worry what kind of day it was going to be. Some running days were magical. On those days I ran faster, felt lighter, floated down a road or a trail almost effortlessly. Other days, I discovered I didn't have it—maybe today, here in the Canyon, was one of those days. The thought was unsettling.

The Pipe Creek Ravine walls expanded further apart as we made our way up the incline. Sometimes I needed to slip behind my new partner, single file where the trail narrowed. The surface was a mix of compacted dirt and stretches composed mostly of rock shards from the Vishnu Schist in a strip down the center.

A burst of lush green vegetation appeared in a descending swath that covered a narrow section of the ravine wall across the way to my right. There was a split here in the cliffside, where water entered Pipe Creek from the bigger Indian Garden stream tributary above and made its way down the rock face, hidden from sight behind the foliage. The result was the little bright green oasis. No doubt the water gushed through when it rained, but now it was a discreet flow. As we continued up the incline and further into the mini-gorge, Pipe Creek—minus its tributary—was reduced to a trickle.

"Do you know what that is over there?" I said.

He turned his head, and I nodded to what looked like a cave at the bottom of the rock wall on the other side of the creek. A dirt path led up to an opening that resembled the Black Bridge tunnel, minus the ring of rocks around the entrance. I'd been tempted to go over to it on my hike, walk inside, and investigate, but I didn't have a flashlight.

"Old mine, I always figured," he said.

"I wonder if it was one of the Ralph Cameron mines. There's a story that he put in claims in order to get the right to charge people a dollar to cross his land on Bright Angel."

"That so?"

Cameron was a Grand Canyon entrepreneur, investor, and eventual Arizona Senator who had obtained control of the early Native American version of the Bright Angel Trail in the 1890s, before almost anyone cared about the Grand Canyon as regards tourism. He built a log-cabin hotel on the South Rim, charged to use the Bright Angel, and further sought to monetize his invest-ment. At one point, Cameron was owner or a partner in close to 40 mining claims that stretched from Jacob's Ladder down through Indian Garden and the Devil's Corkscrew, all the way to the Colo-rado. He was also a partner in the profitable Last Chance copper mine on Horseshoe Mesa at the bottom of the Grandview Trail.

The National Park Service offered to buy him out, and take over the Bright Angel Trail for public use. But Cameron resisted. After he refused an offer of $50,000, the Park Service instead constructed the South Kaibab Trail in the 1920s.

Cameron's hotel went out of business, losing to the more luxurious El Tovar in the competition to attract tourists. He lived until age 89 and is buried on the South Rim at the Pioneer Cemetery near the Canyon Village, in a spot that's marked with a large rock and a plaque.

DEVIL'S CORKSCREW

The gradual upward slope of the Bright Angel Trail came to an abrupt end as we arrived at the Devil's Corkscrew and confronted the rugged, switchback-filled ascent, 1200 feet to the Tonto Platform. I looked up to where we were heading. The Canyon walls rose in layered stages, ever higher, in shades of gray, brown, and rust. I spotted three small figures near the top of the Corkscrew on their way to the Tonto. Given the distance, I couldn't be sure, but they looked like the other three youths.

My newfound partner didn't miss a beat, his cadence maintaining its rhythm. Breathing harder, I jogged up the trail behind him, knees pumping in a truncated stride, like I was hitting Stage Four on a cardiac treadmill test.

The trail here resembled rougher parts of the SK descent—full of exposed cross-trail logs, the surface rutted and worn between them. I put effort into lifting my feet higher, hopping over the logs.

Up ahead of us was a guy with a backpack, using a pair of hiking poles to help propel himself up the trail.

"Comin' through!" my young pal bellowed.

The guy paused and looked at him. "Where's the fire?"

"Just keepin' it movin' for real, dude."

The guy stepped aside.

We continued on our way, with me struggling to keep up. I was starting to seriously sweat. Maybe I should have done more of my training while carrying a full daypack. We moved forward in silence for a few moments. After a couple hundred more yards of toiling up the switchbacks, I gave up running and reverted to power-hiking.

"There you go, dude," he said, glancing back with a smile. "Hiking it ain't so bad."

"I'll run again up on the Tonto."

"Suit yourself."

Meanwhile, I fell into step behind him, trying to match him stride-for-stride. We zigzagged up steep switchbacks. A couple passed us, single file, on their way down, full backpacks laden with their camping gear. We all nodded hello.

At a particularly sharp switchback, the cross-trail logs were again more exposed. Large guide rocks lined either side of the trail. There were a few water breaks to step over, which gave way to a relatively smooth trail as we neared the summit of the Corkscrew. When we reached the top, a pair of jagged rock formations stood like sentries on either side of us. There was a flat area off to the right. I stepped out onto it, put down the daypack, and took a drink of the bottled water, finishing it off.

My companion paused and looked back. "What's up, padre?"

"Do you want to take in the view for a minute?"

"Huh? I guess." He stood there, not removing his backpack, and looked out at the Canyon.

As I also surveyed the terrain, I saw the trail dropping in its snaking switchback descent and the landscape becoming increasingly green the further down I looked. In contrast, there was mostly stark rock around the two of us here. I spotted a few people working their way up Pipe Creek. Below in the distance was a lone guy who could be the fourth youth. The giveaway: He was shirtless.

A few dozen yards down the hillside from us was Garden Creek. I could see where it disappeared, split the rock, and came through on the other side. There, the lush greenery covered the ravine wall, and the water joined up with Pipe Creek.

"Don't suppose you want to take a brief break and go down to the stream? There are some tadpoles I spotted last time on my hike." As soon as I said it, I felt silly.

"That's okay, dude. Need to get up to the rim and phone my girl. Besides, I thought you were in a hurry."

"It'll only take a couple minutes, and frankly, I could use a break."

"You seem fine to me."

"I'm not feeling quite a hundred percent. Not sure what's up." I'd had less than two hours sleep the night before, but I knew that didn't explain it.

"Really? Come on!"

"You should go on ahead."

He took a few steps toward me, standing close.

"Stick with me, and I guarantee you'll hit your time goal."

"Don't know that I can keep up with you."

"Okay," he sighed. "Suit yourself."

"Well, it was good having company."

"Yeah."

"Hey, what's your name?"

"Chris."

I told him mine as we fist-bumped.

"Have a good one," Chris said. He began to stride off. Then, he turned and called back: "Maybe I'll see you up top."

"Maybe."

"Hey." He paused and turned again. "Keep at it, dude. You can be my inspiration for fucking doing this on down the road!"

He headed up the Bright Angel Trail in the direction of Indian Garden. I slipped the empty water bottle into my daypack and watched him go.

CHAPTER 24

NAVIGATING TAPEATS NARROWS

scrambled down the hillside to the creek and placed my day-pack on the bank. Crouching to examine the sunlit pools, I spotted dozens of tadpoles. For a tranquil moment, I watched the little guys squiggle around, the flicking motions of their tails lifting them from place to place as they nibbled algae. Perhaps they were from some of the Spotted or Woodhouse Rocky Mountain toads that inhabited the Canyon. The Canyon tree frog could also be found in the area, but in my experience, tree frog tadpoles were generally brown and fewer in number. These tadpoles were black and plentiful.

In the springtime, when Cassidy and Jamie were younger, I would take them to a stream in Fryman Canyon near our house in Los Angeles. The stream ran year around and must have been fed by a spring somewhere up above, near Mulholland. There was no trail as we made our way up sandbars, climbed over fallen logs and branches, and hiked portions of the bank, until we reached the sunny tadpole pool that was set at the base of a rock face with a sheet of water streaming down. The pool was four or five feet across, a good eight or so inches deep, and full of hundreds of black toad tadpoles with a few tree frog tadpoles mixed in. We sat on the ground and stared into the water, following the movements of the tadpoles, watching them for the first signs of the changes to come.

Ranger Rick mode was, for me, some of my best of times with the girls—sharing, bonding, exploring, teaching them about nature, even if they were growing up in urban Los Angeles. Maybe especially because they were growing up in Los Angeles. I showed them how to identify poison oak with its shiny three-leaf clusters. I pointed out birds: a Spotted Towhee, a California Thrasher with its distinctive downward curved beak, a circling Red-tail hawk. There was other wildlife if we were lucky: a mule deer or a coyote, a rabbit scampering through the brush.

I missed those days. Only Jamie still wanted to join me for an occasional foray into nature. As a teenager, Cassidy was moving on to become her own person. When a child is 15 and on the verge of 16, the family dynamics are in flux, the correct parental moves sometimes hard to divine, the relationship changing. I was trying to adjust, but I didn't know if that was going to be good enough.

We used to bond watching roughcuts of WB shows that I would bring home from the office: *Smallville*, *Buffy*, *Reaper*. Cassidy had a creative side—doing artwork, writing short stories, taking in a variety of television programs, and becoming quite the indie movie buff.

My favorite photo of Cass was the one that appeared on my computer log-in page, showing her draped over my shoulder. It was from a couple years earlier as she taught me the basics of my new laptop—putting her in the driver's seat with her tech know-how. She wasn't a hugger, at least with me, so the fact that she had an arm around me made the photo all the more special.

Today, alone atop the Devil's Corkscrew, I couldn't get too lost examining the tadpoles in Garden Creek. I could only spare a couple minutes. As it was June, I was surprised the tadpoles had yet to begin their metamorphosis. The rear legs would emerge first, sprouting at the base of the tail. Front legs would follow, appearing from the sides of the chest. The head would change its shape, the mouth widening to facilitate a new tongue and a diet of insects. Gills disappeared, lungs developed, and the tadpoles lost the ability to breathe underwater. Instead, their mouths broke the water's surface to gulp oxygen from the world above. They soon emerged onto land as perfectly formed miniature toads, except for their still-intact tails which would quickly vanish, absorbed in a final act of transformation.

I was going through my own transformation: the aging process I was living through. There were mornings when I woke up and felt like I was 25. As if there was absolutely no difference between now and 40 years ago. I was just me. The same me I'd always been. On those mornings, I didn't need coffee first thing when I got out of bed.

Other mornings, I couldn't do without caffeine to function. When I got out of bed, I'd take a moment to compensate for the lower-back crimp or any running-related soreness and felt every bit 64. On the other hand, I refused to use age as an excuse for anything. Just get my ass in gear: Go, do, live life, move forward.

But I never resorted to that trope, "Age is just a number."

It wasn't. And isn't.

I retrieved my daypack, hustled back up the hillside from my brief tadpole visit, and began to run. Here, the Bright Angel Trail was a moderate uphill grade that grew steadily steeper. As I worked my way up, I passed a spot where water came down from a crease in the rocks and crossed the trail on the way to the creek below. I did my best to dodge the worst of the slippery mud.

I hit a stretch that was without guide rocks, despite an abrupt drop to my right several hundred feet straight down. As I circled upward beneath rock promontories, guide rocks reappeared, lining the edge, the running surface relatively smooth for a long section. I focused on lifting one foot before the other, maintaining a slow but steady pace, taking occasional glances out over the Canyon.

Beside the trail, I encountered an Agave plant that stood a good eight feet tall, ramrod-straight, the stalk emerging from a cluster of jagged leaves at its base and blossoming with small yellow flowers. Parts of the plant were edible, including the flowers, and had helped supply the early Native Americans with a food source. The Agave only bloomed once in 15-30 years and died afterwards as its seeds scattered. It reminded me of the also-blooming-only-once Silver Sword plants Kathy and I had seen in Hawaii on the Big Island, the year we visited after losing Josh.

Ensconced in a romantic cottage, we'd focused on achieving success within the several-day pregnancy window. Getting pregnant with Josh had been easy, but creating another child was proving difficult. An early-term miscarriage had crushed our hopes. We were still trying to get pregnant the winter after the Hawaii trip. The location this time was a rustic cabin near the Gallatin River, during a Montana vacation. In between trying to conceive, Kathy taught me to ski on the slopes of the Big Sky Resort, she having come from a Maine family of excellent downhillers.

Cassidy was born eight weeks premature in July 1996, seven months after our Montana trip. We had another infant in the hospital, another round of iso-

Bright Angel Trail
in Tapeats Narrows

lettes, intubation, and NICU (Neonatal Intensive Care Unit), and the attending doctors and nurses. Some members of the medical team had helped Josh, but this time the prognosis was good. Our new baby was home by August—temporarily on an apnea monitor to track her heart rate and breathing, but home all the same.

I rounded a switchback on the Bright Angel past the Agave plant, struggling some with the uphill effort. There were exposed cross-trail logs here. I took a jump over one, then after a couple feet, the next, and another after that. I cut sharply at a switchback which had another sheer drop off the edge and no guide stones lining it, just the trail hanging out over the Canyon. The views were magnificent, but it was best to concentrate on watching my step.

The route crested a summit and became smoother again. I was heading up to Tapeats Narrows, continuing to climb. The trail crossed Garden Creek, which flowed down through the Narrows. I stopped running—glad for the break—and passed over the water on a row of stones. There were cottonwood trees along the stream, which now paralleled the trail. There was also welcoming shade as I entered the Narrows, the route sheltered from sunlight by dark rock walls filled with crevices and fissures on either side of me. Large stone blocks were strewn about. I figured they had either broken off, or they'd been cut from the rock walls to make room for the trail.

The blocks were Tapeats Sandstone, which rested on top of the last of the Vishnu Schist. I was passing through the Great Unconformity again, where the two formations met, and time went missing.

JOY OF RUNNING: IN THE BEGINNING

I was descending switchbacks at a run, trying to put as much distance between myself and the rest of the family as possible. I'd left

     RICK MATER

them behind, still doing their post-picnic packing up, maybe a half-mile back. Continuing to pick up speed, I negotiated the tight turns of the *Col de Tende* pass on the French side of the Maritime Alps.

Our family was halfway through six years of living abroad in Munich, Germany. For my parents, it was a return to the country of their romance. My father, originally from Brooklyn, had served in military intelligence in southern Germany at the end of World War II. My mother had been a liaison officer with the French Army. The two met and fell in love.

Flying down the *Col de Tende* pavement in sandals and lederhosen at age 14, surrounded by mountain peaks, I took an inside track on the hairpin turns, and dodged cars passing me. The more distance I achieved, the better to impress my parents and my two younger brothers with how far and how fast I'd run.

I had thoughts of going out for track or cross country at Munich American High School, where that big blue M on a letter sweater was everything. The school might as well have been located in Kansas, Georgia, or Texas, where some of the military kids were from. Maybe a quarter of us students were civilians whose parents worked for Radio Free Europe, like my father did, or Radio Liberty, Voice of America, or the American consulate.

When it came to sports, I knew that it wasn't going to be baseball for me with childhood memories of misplayed fly balls sailing over my head in right field. Or basketball. I wasn't tall enough or skilled enough. Or football. Not big enough, not good enough. I ended up trying wrestling, where size wasn't an issue, and I wasn't half-bad. Only to be stuck behind the European district champion in my weight class, proud that at least he couldn't pin me in practice.

That left running.

I continued my descent on the *Col de Tende*, the road once an ancient Roman route that meandered its way to the Mediterranean. We were driving to *Les Nefliers*, a small villa located in

Le Cannet, high up in the hills above Cannes. My Grandfather, Henri Blanc had moved there after his retirement from his textile import business in London, returning to his native France.

We kids treasured our visits with Henri. We admired his Légion d'Honneur and Croix de Guerre medals awarded for his World War One service. Mornings, we would watch him head off in his sandals and slacks, carrying his woven shopping bag and walking brusquely down the street to the local cluster of small shops. A filter-less hand-rolled cigarette dangled from his lips as he visited the bakery, the butcher, and for produce, the small grocery store. Sometimes, he let us join him for the little trek.

Once back at the house, Henri would cook up fabulous multi-course feasts. My mother was a very good cook, but she always said she was no match for her father. Her mother Alice—also French—had died of cancer in her 40s, shortly after I was born near their home in Pinner, England. My mother would later worry about cancer when she neared the age at which Alice died. A few years following Alice's death, Henri had remarried.

In the evenings at *Les Nefliers*, my younger brothers and I liked to go through Henri's photo albums with their small black-and-white snapshots of family travels around Europe, and captions done in his meticulous, flowing, fountain-pen cursive. There were photos of my mother, Joan, and her younger brother, Jacques. *Young before we were young, kids before we were kids.* Their parents, Henri and Alice, wore old-fashioned full body-covering bathing suits on various Mediterranean beaches as Joan and Jacques played in the sand.

Henri would respond to our questions about the photos, seemingly surprised at our interest, answering in his gruff, heavily accented French manner, tut-tutting and explaining this or that: "Well, yes, of course, that was Majorca," and "Yes, that was Italy, near . . ." Henry virtually always posed in profile in the photos, staring off somewhere, his Gallic nose prominent. And when he spoke to us, he sounded like the singer and movie star Maurice Chevalier.

Les Nefliers featured a red tile roof, and there were orange and apricot and fig trees on the hillside out back; out front, a huge veranda overlooked the Mediterranean. Cannes was down below, with its fancy tourist hotels, oceanside restaurants, and its famous beaches. The *Boulevard de la Croisette* ran through the heart of it to the marina, with its boats and yachts; in May, there were banners for the annual film festival hung along the route.

The house's veranda with its expansive coastal vistas was where, 30 years later, Kathy and I would sit together and share coffee in the morning during a ten-day stay on our honeymoon. Sadly, Henri was long gone, but his house remained with the English side of my mother's family—my Uncle Jacques and his wife Anne. For my honeymoon with Kathy, we had the run of the place, just the two of us, the house remodeled and updated, but my old memories intact.

As I continued my run down the *Col de Tende*, I turned my head to look for the familiar blue-and-white family Opel Kadet. Where were they? I was starting to tire, and sandals weren't exactly the ideal footwear for running. Finally, I spotted them, working their way down the switchbacks behind me. Knowing I was almost finished, I put on a show for them, running faster until they drove up alongside me. As my mother rolled down the passenger side window, I finally slowed. My father, behind the wheel, brought the car to a stop.

"Well! We were wondering where you were, Richard!" my mother said in her very proper English accent. She was still in her 30s, her face pretty and youthful.

My father was taller than my mother, an imposing 5'11" to her 5'2". At times, he was an authoritarian figure, especially when provoked by my teenage rebelliousness. One of the worst of those instances would occur on this trip at *Les Nefliers*, when he directed me to wash the dishes following one of Henri's feasts. In front of everyone, I told my father, "Do it yourself!" Then, I retreated through the kitchen door and up to the safety of the orchard on the hill out back, watching from above as he called to me and ordered that I come down.

"No," I answered. Finally, after a suitable amount of time elapsed, I made my way downhill to the house, figuring rightly that corporal punishment would be limited this time—or even off the table completely, due to the presence of relatives.

Alternately, my father tried to bond with me over just-the-two-of-us Sunday drives back in Germany. On the drive, we'd often stop at a *Landgasthaus* for a lunch of *Wienerschnitzel, Kartoffel Salad, Apfelsaft,* and a cake or ice cream dessert—a bribe of sorts by my father. Words of wisdom flowed from him as we drove: soliloquys about goals, achievement, striving, conformity in service of career.

On that long-ago day in the Maritime Alps, after my father pulled over to pick me up, I took my regular seat behind him. My brother Philip, five years younger than me, sat in the middle. My other brother Gene, a year-and-a-half my junior, sat to Philip's right.

"You must be tired," my father said. Despite his seeming concern, I knew all he truly cared about was my academic standing at school. He showed zero interest in my pursuing any athletic endeavors.

"No, I'm fine," I said to him as we continued along the highway to Le Cannet.

Philip's death: a construction incident. A fatal 40-foot fall from a roof being installed with no safety harness provided to him and the other workers. Dead at 43 in 1996.

Thankfully, my mother hadn't lived to suffer the death of her youngest son—or of Josh. I'd rushed to visit my parents at their later-life home in Charlottesville, Virginia, a couple years before Philip died—pushed by Kathy's alarm at what was going on with my mother's pulmonary problems. Upon my arrival, I was stunned at my mother's appearance. Her hair was a shocking white. She pulled around a portable oxygen tank with a rubber tube running up to a nasal cannula to aid her breathing. Through it all, she persevered, her outward demeanor appearing as if she was just dealing with some sort of normal obstacle in life.

My father was in denial at the seriousness of it all, having lived through the slow minor changes, the day-to-day progression, seemingly unaware of—or unwilling to face—the alarming state of things. While there, I played them a videocassette of baby Josh at home with us in Los Angeles during the hopeful interlude before he went back to the hospital.

The next time I visited Charlottesville, my mother's body was lying in an open casket at a funeral home. Alone with her for a moment in a side room before the memorial service began, I wasn't sure what to say or do. Take a photo with the camera I had with me? No, that was crazy. I stepped a bit closer—but not truly close—and stood there looking at her in repose, my eyes damp.

Had I ever told her that I loved her? I wasn't sure. Had she said it to me? I didn't think so, at least not since I was very young. I had no memory of it. Even physical touching was limited mostly to polite hello hugs and goodbye hugs, ours not a tactile family; public displays of emotions were held in check.

When it came to speaking publicly about my mother, I was too overwhelmed to say anything at the small, intimate service that started a few minutes later. My father was in even worse shape. My brother Gene was left to handle the speaking duties, which he did with aplomb and sensitivity.

Josh followed my mother in death a few months later at Thanksgiving.

Three deaths in two years: my mother, Josh, and Philip.

Now, I spoke to my mother during my Sunday runs, high up on the Ridge Trail, wishing that she was still alive. She would have savored every precious minute she could have spent with Cassidy and Jamie—cursed with the bad fortune to have three sons, not the daughter that she craved.

She could have provided the girls with precious memories of their grandmother. They would never get to know her beyond photos and a snippet from our wedding video when she'd responded to some question from me in her still-accented way.

In six years, I would be the same age my mother was when she died—and battling my own cardiac-related issues.

Tick, tick, tick.

DEPARTING THE NARROWS

I continued at a slow, steady run, ascending back up through time. As I made my way to the upper part of Tapeats Narrows, the sides of the ravine came closer together. The trail here was rocky and uneven underfoot. There were step-ups as the route climbed, and I had to jump onto each one, watching my footing. There were more scattered blocks around me, a section of the rock sandstone wall fracturing and sliding into the Canyon.

The Tapeats Sandstone was the first of the layers of geologic formations piled atop the jumble of the Great Unconformity and the Vishnu Schist. Formed by layers of sediment from the warm, shallow seas that once covered this area, the sandstone was the oldest unit of the Tonto Group. At the time, this land was located near the South Pole on the continent of Laurentia, which was part of the supercontinent of Pannotia that preceded Pangea.

The Narrows constricted further as I ran. There were more cottonwoods along the creek. In the Canyon, the trees only grew where there was permanent water. There were willows here as well, and even a small waterfall cascading into a pool.

I imagined that when it rained, the creek's noisy rushing sounds magnified as it echoed between the walls of the Narrows. The trail had clearly been constructed above the creek to keep it passable during flooding.

At the waterfall, the rock wall on the other side of the ravine from me radically changed appearance. The sandstone layers became thin and stacked like pancakes, appearing almost volcanic, as if each overlay had oozed out in a molten lava flow, cooled, and froze in place. Then, another sheet formed on top of it, and another, and another, creating a series of dramatic terraced ledges.

Around a bend, the trail returned to dirt, and a few semi-submerged cross-trail logs appeared. I kept running at a slow jog, lifting my feet just enough to clear the logs and the various rocks, in order to avoid a stumble.

Two guys—likely in their 30s, loaded down with camping backpacks, and utilizing hiking poles—headed toward me. They moved into single file and nodded a greeting as we passed one another.

Running from the top of the Corkscrew, up through the Narrows to Indian Garden, had not seemed unreasonable to me in my planning—until now. I started to tire noticeably and briefly switched to power-hiking again.

CHAPTER 25

INDIAN GARDEN

I came striding out of the Narrows into an open area. A solitary cottonwood tree appeared, full and leafy green. A sign to my right announced, "INDIAN GARDEN"—the letters black, as if burned into the weathered wood. An arrow below the words pointed straight ahead. I resumed running, faster now, as if nearing an imaginary finish line. It was a trick I used on my long Sunday runs, late into them, trying to manufacture some speed and get me to the end with at least some semblance of my younger, faster self.

Another rustic wood sign appeared: "TONTO EAST." The narrow ribbon of the Tonto Trail came in on my left, arriving after a winding four and a half miles from where I'd crossed it at the Tip Off. If you so chose, you could skip going all the way to the bottom of the Canyon and, instead, traverse the Tonto between Indian Garden and the Tip Off. That stretch, linking the Bright Angel and the South Kaibab, was the only section of the Tonto with any foot traffic to speak of. But even so, you could hike or run it and still not encounter a soul. The Canyon was like that: Phantom Ranch and Bright Angel Campground busy with people, versus utter isolation elsewhere—sometimes on the same trail, depending on the time of day, the season, or the difference of just a mile or two.

As I ran up past the Tonto junction, the Bright Angel Trail became smooth sand-colored dirt and easy to navigate. The vegetation was increasingly lush around me, even more so than in Tapeats Narrows. I could see the Redwall limestone cliff ahead and up above, looming majestically, the morning sun turning it scarlet. It was part of the same formation I'd encountered below Skeleton Point on the descent. Indian Garden would be below it.

I came upon the back of a metal sign. I knew that it was another of the warnings featuring the outline of the parched hiker clad in shorts and a T-shirt—this one to convince people coming down Bright Angel on a casual day hike to turn around if they ventured beyond Indian Garden. I wasn't feeling too great myself. This stretch of the route felt like it was taking forever. Where was Indian Garden?

On my left, the small stone building that served as the pumping station for the Trans-Canyon Pipeline was partially obscured by trees and brush. I was getting closer. A stand of cottonwoods materialized enticingly up ahead, their crowns pointing the way.

With relief, I jogged into the shady retreat of Indian Garden—finally. Plopping down on the nearest bench, I stretched my legs, leaned back, and let my daypack drop beside me.

A 30-something woman sat on the next bench over, munching some trail mix.

"Excuse me," I said. "Can you tell me the time?"

"Sure," she said, checking a wrist. "8:42."

"Thanks."

It had taken me just short of two hours to make it up from Phantom Ranch—roughly what I'd allowed for, even with more power-hiking than I'd anticipated. So far, so good. Regardless of not feeling one hundred percent I was still on pace to break six hours. I had two hours left to accomplish that, with four-plus miles and 3000-plus feet of elevation gain to go.

I gazed around. Indian Garden had the appearance of a rustic retreat. People were resting on benches, sitting on rocks, and kicking back. Some were talking, taking a break with backpacks at their feet. The ones on the way down exuded a more relaxed air and lacked the serious sweat of exertion. Perhaps there were a dozen folks in all. A few gathered around a water spigot and filled containers. So much for any water supply issues; the pipeline obviously repaired and working.

There were more of the cottonwoods here, with their rough, deeply furrowed bark and fans of branches and leaves amid the trails and paths leading in various directions. A small bathroom building across from me was built in the motif of Mary Colter's Phantom Ranch design: stone walls and a green roof with teal wood trim. There was also a marked emergency phone, mule tie-ups, and a roof-covered display with maps and information.

I could make out tents in bright colors through the brush. There was a campground at Indian Garden. If you signed up early enough, there were 37 permits for camping spaces. Some included a picnic table located underneath a four-posted wooden roof to provide sun and rain protection. *Death in Grand Canyon* told the story of a young guy camping here who woke up to take a pee in the dark and fell to his death when he accidentally stepped off the edge.

Chris the Hiker Dude was nowhere to be seen, which was hardly a surprise. I wondered how far up he was. I imagined him passing hikers bewildered by the sound of his approaching pounding feet and a hearty "Coming through!" if they dawdled in stepping aside.

"Can you watch my pack for a moment?" I said to the woman who'd told me the time.

"Sure," she replied.

I got up and walked over to the temperature gauge situated at the north end of the resting area. It was a glass-covered display, with a ring of numbers from -60 to 120. A twin of the thermometer at the Bright Angel campground footbridge, it was likewise mounted on a post, except this one had a wooden sign immediately below it that said, "THIS IS YOUR BRAIN ON SUN." An arrow above the words directed your eye up to the thermometer. The red dial pointed to 80 degrees. I was glad I'd escaped the inner gorge early, where it was likely already 90. But 80 wasn't any treat either, and it would soon be getting hotter.

I returned to the bench.

"Thanks," I said to the woman.

"No problem."

I took a water bottle and a peanut butter-and-honey sandwich out of my daypack. The sandwich seemed unappetizing, and I still wasn't hungry, so I put it back in the pack. I had a sip from the new bottle of water, gathered my things, looking around to be sure I had it all in the drill to which I had recently become accustomed.

As I got older, I had to start paying attention to all sorts of little things that had once been second nature. This was especially true as I moved about from one place to another. Leaving for the morning commute in L.A: Reading glasses in shirt pocket? Check. Wallet in back pocket? Check. BlackBerry in its holder clipped to my belt? Check. Car keys? Check. Cell phone inside pants pocket? Check. Work ID in shirt pocket? Check.

The checklist drill had become *de rigueur* after I'd suffered through annoying mental glitches that I attributed to aging, such as leaving my BlackBerry at the security conveyer belt at LAX and having to run back in a panic after being halfway to the boarding gate. Thankfully, TSA was holding on to it.

Or mysteriously losing my reading glasses somewhere at a hotel in Boston when I took Jamie to summer camp in Vermont. For the life of me, I couldn't find them anywhere, and—my 20/20 vision a thing of the past—I'd reached the point where reading glasses had become a necessity, not an option. The solution was a quick trip to the drugstore across the street to pick up a cheap replacement pair.

But the thing that drove me the craziest? My damn credit card. I left it behind at a restaurant more than once, and each time, I was relieved to find out they had it. And there were the times I started to leave it at a store with a "You forgot your card, sir!" from the checkout person stopping me in my tracks.

When you were younger, momentary forgetfulness was nothing—just an annoying slip of the mind. But years later, it became something else entirely: a disturbing symptom of aging, part of the systemic decline of your senses, a loss of situational awareness and mental crispness. Not to mention that I could be experiencing some leading indicator of dementia. There was, after all, also the question of whether Alzheimer's was in my future, with the history of the disease in the family and my mysterious inability to recognize where I was on that Fryman Canyon run. And there was my wrong turn at Cedar Ridge today. None of it boded well for the inevitability of me becoming truly "old."

Were these perhaps the last of the best of times? The future to be navigated with a need to craft a new vision of my life. In five years, when my daughters would be beginning to leave home and move on with their lives—going to college and then the rest of it—I would be 69. In ten years, I would be 74 and, I expected, no longer gainfully employed . . . *Jesus, what then?*

It was time to get moving.

I spotted the three young guys, standing perhaps 30 feet away to my left, where there was a small step up to a second tree-shaded clearing. They were talking, casting glances in my general direction, and likely anticipating the arrival of their straggling friend somewhere on the route behind me. It looked like they were preparing to head out.

I double-checked around me on the bench, got up, slung my daypack from a shoulder by a single strap, and walked towards them.

"Not waiting up for your friend?" I said.

"Oh. Have you seen Francisco?" It was the guy who'd been in front at Phantom Ranch and seemed to be in charge.

"Yeah, back on the River Trail. He was taking a break and told me you guys were going to meet up here."

"We've been waiting for at least half an hour," said the one in the ASU cap.

"I think we should try to maybe wait a few minutes more," said the tall one who was carrying the daypack and who I knew from Francisco to be Bernardo.

"He can't be too far behind me," I said. "The last time I saw him, he was coming up Pipe Creek."

"Well, we're going to all end up at the same place—at the rim," said the leader. "Maybe if you see him, you can tell him we're heading out. See him up top."

"Okay. Sure."

"Let's go, guys." Turning back to me, he said, "Well, have a good hike."

"Oh, I'm running it—like you guys." I managed a smile. "Well, maybe a little slower."

They appeared surprised.

"I mean, most of it," I added. "Jacob's Ladder is pretty much impossible to run."

"We'll see about that," said the leader.

"Oh, you've done it before?"

"No," he admitted. "Let's go, guys," he repeated.

I watched them run single file as they left.

"Good luck," I called after them.

Bernardo looked back. "Nice meeting you, sir," he said.

I cringed at "sir."

Well, I'd caught them, which made me feel good. Except that it didn't really count. After all, they'd been waiting around for a half-hour. Otherwise, they would be well ahead of me. But if I was to catch them *again* up ahead, that would truly mean something. Jacob's Ladder could be the great equalizer—it was virtually impossible to run.

I started hiking uphill through the rest of Indian Garden. On my right, a burnished wood sign on a low post announced: "PLATEAU POINT 1.5 MI." Under that it said, "TONTO WEST," and directed you back down to where the Tonto, the longest trail in the Canyon, resumed its 95-mile journey after its brief merger with the Bright Angel. If you descended to the Tonto junction and continued a half-mile-plus past it, you reached the Plateau Point cul-de-sac where, at the edge of the gorge, that suicide leap documented in *Death in Grand Canyon* had occurred.

But for me, today was feeling more about life.

The vegetation eased up as the Bright Angel Trail resumed out of Indian Garden—initially, a modest incline of pinkish dirt marked by rocks on either side and surrounded by rust-brown Canyon. Three thousand-plus feet above me, I could see the South Rim, demarcated against the sky, its whitish-gray Kaibab Limestone topped with rock formations that resembled turrets on a distant castle wall.

ANOTHER ANGIOPLASTY—AUGUST 2011

"Don't die in the Grand Canyon, Dad!" Jamie said to me, a few weeks before I was due to depart for my planned Canyon practice hike with my older cousin James. Those plans hit a snag when

Jamie brought me up short with her plea. She'd already confided to Kathy and me about a dream she had that I would die when she was 15. Perhaps this was a result of her being traumatized by my emergency angioplasty when she was 6 years old. I didn't believe in that sort of premonition but still made a mental note it gave me four more years.

"I've been thinking about that, Jamie" I said. "I'll move up my annual treadmill test."

"But you only have a few weeks until the hike," she said.

"I'm on it. I promise I'll get the test first."

Soon, I was briskly walking along—not in the Grand Canyon but hooked up to an EKG. I was wearing my running shorts, a faded 10K race T-shirt, my Asics keeping up with the rubber pad in motion beneath my feet.

There had first been a resting echocardiogram done with a handheld ultrasound unit that checked my chest and heart as I lay on an exam table. This process would be repeated after my exercise exertion.

The first of the three-minute treadmill stages was easy. There was a blood pressure check at the two-minute mark, administered by a male medical technician in brown scrubs with a nurse practitioner standing close by in a white smock. The med tech wrapped a leather cuff around my right arm and squeezed the hand pump to make it contract snug against my bicep. The blood pressure results were visible next to me on a monitor.

Stage Two followed for another three minutes, with a low uphill tilt to the treadmill, a faster walking pace, and another blood pressure test.

Stage Three required striding along at a good clip, the tilt steeper, with still another blood pressure check.

"Okay, in 30 seconds, we're moving it up to the next level," said the nurse practitioner.

"Sure," I said, gripping the waist-high bar in front of me, continuing to stride along. With a whirring noise, the treadmill rose up under me for Stage Four, the angle steeper, and I started running in place.

"You're in good shape," the nurse practitioner said as I thumped away. "Most people don't make it this far. Let's see if we can get your pulse up to the 160 target."

I glanced over at the monitor. It registered 120.

"It might take a while. I'm a runner," I said.

"Really?" It was the med tech.

"Yeah, I ran 11 miles up on Mulholland yesterday." The run had gone okay, but I'd also taken a one-minute walking break after each mile, which was unusual. Back in June, I'd had a bad crash-and-burn eight-miler up there that was so subpar it made me wonder if something was up.

"Wow!" said the male tech.

I continued for another couple minutes, pounding away on the treadmill. The med tech skipped the blood pressure check this time.

"We're going to the next setting," the nurse practitioner said.

I glanced over again. My pulse was 138. I was starting to sweat. I didn't feel so great.

"This next stage should get you to 160."

"Okay," I said, preparing for the added exertion as we hit Stage Five. I clung some to the bar now, my grip tighter; the tilt of the treadmill rose steeper still, my sweating became more pronounced, my knees churned faster. I hoped we'd finish soon but was reluctant to give the word to stop. Perhaps I shouldn't have boasted about running Mulholland.

"Almost," the nurse practitioner said. "We're about to hit 160. Just another minute—if you're okay with it. Or would you like to stop?"

"I'll just kept running," I said, and I soldiered on for another 20 or 30 seconds before I said finally, "I'm ready to stop."

"Okay, we just hit 160. Get ready. We're slowing it down."

I switched to walking as the treadmill slowed and came to a stop. The male tech hustled me back over to the exam table, where he had me rest on my side as he conducted another chest exam with the handheld ultrasound. Then, he unhooked me from the EKG, unstrapping the belt from my waist; he removed the wires connecting to the sticky contacts affixed to my body, followed by the contacts themselves.

"How'd I do?" I asked the nurse practitioner.

"You'll need to get the results from the doctor," she said crisply. "Please sit down for five minutes and drink some juice before you leave. You can have a cookie."

The conversation with Doctor Stephens was not long in coming. He was about ten years my junior, with wire rim glasses and a perpetually earnest demeanor—other than a brief smile he sometimes permitted himself after an appointment was almost concluded. We sat opposite each other in a small exam room in the same medical complex in Burbank as the treadmill test. He was in one chair. I was in another.

"Sorry, the news isn't good. Your EKG results, while not conclusive, indicate something irregular. I'm ordering you an angiogram to find out more about what's going on. We can fit you in in two weeks. If it confirms my suspicions, you'll need to go straight into another angioplasty."

"But it's only been four years," I protested. Truthfully, I'd been warned when I had my first angioplasty that this could happen.

"Well, I'm sorry, but that's what we are dealing with," Doctor Stephens continued. "I'm afraid it goes without saying that you'll have to cancel your Grand Canyon plans."

"Postpone," I said.

"Alright, postpone."

"What about my regular running?"

"I can't stop you. Keep it slow and easy, and you know my cautions. Watch for any symptoms: chest pain, shortness of breath, heart palpitations, feeling faint. And stay hydrated. It's August, for Pete's sake."

The angiogram was an X-ray of my chest, with iodine dye injected into the blood vessels for a coronary diagnostic that would check for blockages. After it was completed, Kathy and I sat with Doctor Stephens in a room at Saint Joseph's Hospital in Burbank.

"You're back to 80% occluded in your left anterior descending aorta," Doctor Stephens said. "It's in between two of your previous stents, so you'll need another angioplasty and a fourth stent. We'll prep you, and you'll spend the night here."

"Really? It's almost back to what it was the first time?"

"I'm afraid so."

"So, I've been running on this?"

"Yes, at least since the day of the treadmill test. There's no way of knowing how long it's been obstructed."

"Jesus. I ran an 11-miler in the hills the day before the test."

Doctor Stephens shook his head. "You keep beating the odds, my friend."

Then, I thought about the impact of the angioplasty on my plans to trial hike the Canyon, factoring in a few weeks of recovery and reduced running. With snow, mud, and storms, the South Kaibab and Bright Angel would effectively rule out running for the winter. I would need to try again the following year in the spring or early summer. Reluctantly, I would have to cancel my late September reservation at the Maswick Lodge and my plans to meet up with my cousin and his friends.

I read over the medical waiver saying I understood that, should something go wrong, the procedure could be fatal. I signed it and the rest of the paperwork and had another angioplasty.

CHAPTER 26

THREE MILE REST HOUSE

I came hiking up the Bright Angel Trail leaving Indian Garden. I paused to put my arms through the straps of the daypack, secured it against my shoulders, and started to run. For the most part, the trail was smooth and easy to manage, as I headed up just east of the Redwall Formation cliff.

More cottonwood trees were on my right, strung out along the water flowing from the spring that was the source for Garden Creek. On my left was a sharp hillside, partly covered in low brush. Clusters of prickly pear cactus grew on either side of the trail, some waist high and some even reaching my chest. A month earlier, they'd been blossoming yellow and purple flowers—small, precious bursts of color interrupting the mostly sparse landscape.

There was also a low, split rail wooden fence running alongside me. Beyond the fence, the Indian Garden Ranger Station was visible, an American flag hanging on a pole beside it. The modest one-story structure included some of the familiar Mary Colter Phantom Ranch design elements.

The cottonwoods petered out and the fence came to an end as the trail veered to the left and began to steepen. The cactus clusters ended as well. The trail widened to maybe eight feet across for a stretch, followed by a return to the more typical narrower route. There were periodic stone cross-trail log equivalents, rectangular and angling across the way, but close to flush with the surface and easy to navigate. I could see switchbacks looming up ahead as the crux of the climb began.

A few day hikers passed me as they descended; some serious backpackers were mixed in as well, hunkered down with their gear. I increased my effort as the trail angled higher, a forward lean to my body as if I was running into a wind, the daypack tight against my shoulders. The Trans-Canyon Pipeline also continued its journey; a section of it was visible, mounted via stone supports as it accompanied me on its way to service the Three Mile Rest House, the Mile and a Half Rest House, and the lodges and restaurants up on the rim.

A series of exposed cross-trail logs appeared, and I jumped up and over, each jump more difficult. I was just barely clearing them. Guide rocks lined both sides of the route, the ones on the inside marking a foot-deep channel for rain runoff, the ones on the outside delineating varying degrees of drop off.

I'd had a fantasy of running most of the way from Indian Garden to the Three Mile Rest House—one and a half miles up the daunting switchbacks of Jacob's Ladder—before making the transition to power-hiking for the last of it, which was the hardest part of the entire route. Running it slowly, to be sure, in a shuffling jog necessitated by the sheer climb. Not much faster really than doing it at a solid power-hike, but running it all the same.

I hit a sharp switchback with more low guide stones. The stones soon came to an end at a perilous, unmarked stretch of drop-off. It was hard to figure out how the placement of the guide stones had been determined, given that they were sometimes present in benign spots and absent in the most dangerous of places.

I reached a portion of trail thrown into shade. It immediately felt as if the temperature dropped by 10 degrees, as I continued my slow-motion run upward. The route continued alternating between sun and shade. At each switchback, the entirety of the way travelled up from Indian Garden was laid out for me below.

Finally, overcome with exhaustion, I changed to power-hiking again, actually gaining speed. The turns grew tighter, the Bright Angel Trail rougher as it whipsawed up the Redwall Formation. There wasn't the dramatic cliff here like the one that rose off to my right and loomed over Indian Garden; rather, the formation was an eroded rocky slope speckled with brush and juniper trees.

More rock water breaks appeared, bordered by foot-high oblong stones on either side, and I stepped up and over each one. This section of the trail looked like it was straight out of the toughest of the South Kaibab's descent: cross-trail logs fully exposed, a ladder of them leading uphill. The route here bore signs that it became a stream in the rain; places were still damp, with rocks scattered about, piles of dried mud, and gouged-out areas along the inside of the way.

I paused for a moment, placed my daypack on the ground, and took a drink of water from a fresh bottle. It was warm from the day heating up around me. I wondered about what was going on with my body. My legs felt beyond tired, and so did the rest of me. Was it fatigue? Was it something more serious that hadn't yet fully manifested itself? A medical issue that could worsen the further up I went and the more stressful the climb became?

"Stroke out" had entered my lexicon when Kathy used it in connection with me running the Canyon. Her medical background as an RN prompted warnings born of her worst-case-scenario medical knowledge.

"You could stroke out!" she said to me. "Or worse, have a stroke *and live*. Do you want to spend the rest of your life in a wheelchair?"

"I could have a stroke just sitting at my desk at work," I said.

"The odds are worse engaging in strenuous activity," she answered. Then, she added a favorite Maine saying of hers: "Running the Grand Canyon is a *fool-killer*, you know."

Her comments were a far cry from "I'm not done with you!" and "I love you, I love you, I love you" as they wheeled me into the OR for my emergency angioplasty five years earlier. The 12-year age difference between us was becoming more of an issue since the advent of my cardiac history.

I wondered what awaited me on the rim when I called home, and tomorrow upon my return to Los Angeles—having disregarded the wishes of the family and the recommendation of Doctor Stephens. I told myself I needed to focus more on my family, on Kathy, going forward. But all too often, I was filled with good intentions and failed at following through.

I would ignore the physical discomfort as much as possible for now, including what it might mean medically. This was my current state of being, after all—living with the realization that, at any moment, things could go south to a nasty conclusion. My new normal. While my medical history made whatever I was currently feeling a cause for potential alarm, that same medical history made me almost blasé at times. Fatalistic even. Running with four stents was just a fact of my life. The once unimaginable now so much a part of my existence that I often forgot about it.

I twisted the cap back on the water bottle, retrieved the daypack, and went back to power-hiking. Looking at the route ahead of me as it zigzagged skyward, I could just make out what must be the three young guys on a switchback up above as they negotiated it at a run. They had slowed noticeably from their pace out of

Indian Garden but were still in close formation and moving along at a solid clip.

I thought again how there should be a big, fat reset button that you could punch at age 60. A button that would send you back in time to start over again. Say to age 18, just as you were deciding what college to attend, but with the hindsight provided by a life already lived. Maybe change your school, change your major, improve your performance in your various pursuits—academic, social, sports. Do that year abroad this time. Get a second chance to determine your future direction in life. Plus, inhabit a younger version of your body that could jump higher, run faster, endure more abuse.

In six months, I would need to sign up for Medicare, no matter that I wouldn't be using it anytime soon. I had medical insurance through my job. I'd also been filling out paperwork for pensions from my stints at media companies: six years at NBC and 13 years combined at the WB Network and its successor, the CW.

A copy of *Social Security for Dummies* sat unopened on a shelf at the house. I had no plans to retire, especially with the kids still in high school and middle school respectively, and no desire for change and a transition to the next stage of my life—*whatever the hell that was going to be.*

As I crested a sun-exposed switchback and the trail leveled off, I was able to manufacture a labored jog. I could see the Three Mile Rest House just ahead, perched on its rocky slope, surrounded by scattered juniper trees. I picked up my pace, the Rest House now another make-believe-end-of-a-race goal in my head in order to produce a little more speed. While that worked on training runs back in L.A. and in races, it quickly became apparent speed was not in the cards at this point today. I just needed to will myself to get there—no matter if I could only do so at the slowest of jogs.

A pile of stones at a trail spur on my left marked my arrival, along with multiple wooden signs: "3 M. HOUSE," "EMERGENCY PHONE," "RESTROOMS," and the all-important "WATER." A fancier, bigger sign on twin posts was mounted just behind the others, facing day-hikers coming down the Bright Angel; it featured a color photo of the Canyon as a backdrop and warned, "To reduce your risk of needing rescue: STOP, REST, HYDRATE, EAT, SAFETY, EVALUATE, HAZARD." An alert in a yellow diamond portion of the sign gave a reminder of the climb back out to come:

"CAUTION!
Down is optional.
UP IS
MANDATORY"

I hooked left and hiked up 10 or 15 yards of smooth dirt. Before I reached the Rest House, I spotted a spigot mounted atop a pipe. Several people were gathered around to refill their water containers, the ground wet from spills. I got in line, emptied the bottle I'd been drinking from, and refilled it with cool water from the spigot.

The Rest House stood at the top of the incline. Perhaps "house" was too grandiose a description for the crude stone shelter—a hut-like structure that featured a peaked roof supported by columns of stacked, un-mortared rocks. A series of rough stone steps led up to it. I grabbed a spot inside and sat down.

"Excuse me," I said to a guy near me. "Do you know what time it is?"

"Sure," he said, checking his wrist. "It's 9:23."

I thanked him.

It had taken me about 40 minutes to make it the mile and a half from Indian Garden to the Rest House. My pace had been steady if unremarkable and frankly, given the steepness of the grade, not a lot slower than if I'd run the entirety of the stretch. I had an hour and 21 minutes left to finish the remaining three miles to the rim. Breaking six hours was still within reach. I needed to keep my pause brief.

I looked around. Just beyond the shelter, there were bathrooms—more of the outhouses with pit toilets—available in a brown wooden structure. Behind the bathrooms, a spit of trail led to a stunning view from a sheer rock cliff that dropped straight down at least 100 feet without so much as a railing. I'd visited it on my training hike. The fearless—or foolish—made their way even further out to a rocky point, with steep drops on either side, for a risky photo op.

Across the way from the rocky point was a butte known as the Battleship, which culminated in a summit strikingly similar in appearance to O'Neill Butte. Comprised of blocks of Supai Group stone stacked up into a narrow, nearly flat cap, the Battleship was so named because the top—which rose to 5850 feet—resembled the bridge of a warship.

A few adventurous people liked to hike over to the Battleship from the Bright Angel at about the two-mile mark from the rim where, at a wide switchback, there was an unmarked side trail. Not for the faint of heart, it was a barely a trail at all. The route required that you bushwhack your way across the Hermit Shale and clamber up a chute called the Chimney, which was clogged with loose rock broken off from the butte. A guy had died when he slipped and fell while climbing inside the Chimney, trapped there and alone. Once atop the Battleship, the views were no doubt spectacular: the Bright Angel snaking below, Indian Garden further, the vastness of the Canyon spread out before you.

Following a couple minutes in the Rest House out of the sun, I got to my feet, hoisted my daypack and, carrying the bottled water in my hand, headed out. I walked back down the spur, reached the Bright Angel Trail, and was surprised to see Francisco hiking up toward me.

"You made it!" I said to him.

"Oh, hi," he said as he came to a stop, looking up at me, and breathing hard. "Yeah."

"I ran into your pals at Indian Garden. Bernardo wanted to wait for you, but the leader guy was in a hurry and—"

"The leader guy?" Francisco laughed. "You mean Eduardo? About my height? Kinda pushy?"

"Sounds like him."

"He's my cousin."

"Well, they're up ahead, still running. I spotted them a few minutes ago."

"That's great, but I really need some water," he said.

"I'll see you again, I expect," I said as he hiked around me.

I turned onto Bright Angel and gave running a try again. Just keep moving, I told myself. In the back of my mind was the thought of maintaining a lead on Francisco, no matter how I was feeling.

SIX MONTHS TO LIVE

Some days more than others, it felt like it was simply a matter of time. How long did I have left? Six years? Six months? Six days? Six hours? Six minutes? Suppose it was in fact six months and I knew that for sure. What would I do? What would *you* do if you found out you had six months to live?

Presumably, the enlightened answer would be that you wouldn't change a thing. You were *already* leading a fulfilling, purposeful life that made you happy, or mostly happy—or at least not profoundly *unhappy*. You might move a few items up the bucket list. Perhaps you'd get some things off your chest to loved ones and friends, not leave important things unsaid. Maybe you'd do some extra travel and take that vacation you had been putting off. Quit your job if you hated it; maybe even if you didn't.

You can find anything online, including people responding to the six-months-to-live question.

Somebody said they would just live their normal daily life with the people they loved. One person posted that they would go off and camp in a forest, commune with nature, and invite their friends to come by. Another said they'd be sad because of regrets they had. Someone else proclaimed they would stop caring about what other people thought and become fearless in how they lived their life.

One more wondered, "what if you change six months to 60 years?"

CHAPTER 27

MILE AND A HALF REST HOUSE

I felt like I was running in slow motion. My pace had been reduced to a shuffling gait. Here, the Bright Angel was as treacherous for running as the South Kaibab in its most dangerous places. Even going *up* was tricky, with ladders of rutted cross-trail logs, stone water breaks, and the unevenness of the path.

I paused and took a sip from my bottle. The water was already growing warm. I would refill it at the Mile and a Half Rest House. I peered back at the Canyon vistas with weary amazement at the elevation gain I'd achieved since the river. Then, I went back to power hiking mixed with sporadic attempts at a jog. Just up ahead, I could see the three young guys. They were no longer running; they were hiking, their configuration ragged. I rounded the next switchback, and there they were, resting on rocks in the shade thrown by the uphill side of the trail.

I'd caught them for real this time.

"Hey, sir. Did you see Francisco?" It was Bernardo who was sitting on a large rock along with ASU Guy. Eduardo was on another rock near them.

"Yep. Back at the Three Mile Rest House," I said as I reached them. I tried not to let on how bad I was feeling. "He should be right behind me." They looked down the trail, and I turned my head as well, but there was no sign of Francisco.

I noticed that the purple water container rested across Eduardo's lap, its top open and the lid dangling from its plastic connector. There was sweat gleaming on his brow and on his bare chest.

"Would you like a bottled water? I've got an extra. It's warm by now, but it's still water."

Eduardo hesitated and then said, "Sure, man."

I pulled one of the three remaining bottles out of my daypack and handed it to him. My generosity was tempered by being glad to lighten my load.

Eduardo unscrewed the cap, poured half the water into his purple container, and passed the partially drained bottle to ASU Guy who took a couple gulps and, in turn, gave it to Bernardo.

"We're not too far from the Mile and a Half Mile Rest House," I said to Bernardo as he polished off the water. "You can refill there."

"Thanks," he said.

"Well, I better get going."

"You got a bus to catch?" Eduardo said, and he laughed. I had the thought that he cared about me getting ahead of them and was perhaps annoyed by the idea. Truthfully, I was making sure to leave first. I hoped the next place I would see them was on the South Rim, struggling up behind me.

"Well, I have that time goal," I said.

"Time goal?"

"Yeah. Remember, I want to do this in under six hours."

"You're crazy," he said, shaking his head. "Besides, you don't look so good. How old are you, anyway?"

"Old enough."

"Yeah," said ASU Guy. "I bet you're old enough to—"

"—be your grandfather," I said.

"Well, maybe not *that* old."

"I'm 64."

"Wow," said Bernardo. "My pops is 40, and my grandpops is, I think, 62."

Nobody said anything for a moment. The number of day hikers heading down was picking up. Three guys passed us, followed by a solo woman. I noticed that she wore a wide-brimmed hat and hiking boots, and she carried a CamelBak hydration system with its tube for sucking water while on the move. At least some people came prepared.

"Well, it's really time to get going," I said. "I'm sure we'll be seeing each other again." I retrieved my daypack and slung it over a shoulder.

"Dudes!" It was Francisco, hiking up towards us.

"Hey," I called to him, and I got going. I slow jogged until I was out of their sight and switched to hiking. I passed a spur on my left that I remembered from my hike partway down Bright Angel with Jamie two years earlier. During our trek, I'd spotted discarded camping gear on the spur that someone apparently decided wasn't worth the effort of hauling the rest of the way up to the rim. I'd gone over to investigate, Jamie following me, in order to make sure there wasn't someone in distress. The spur quickly came to a dead end, no one in sight.

Continuing on our way down the Bright Angel, I'd stopped Jamie.

"I think we need to go back," I said. Jamie was wearing light blue shorts, a T-shirt, and a sun hat. I'd been enforcing Kathy's sunblock mandate, insisting that my daughter apply a decent amount while in our room at the Maswick Lodge inside the park.

"That's Indian Garden, right?" Jamie said.

Upper Bright Angel Trail

I looked down to where she was pointing below us. "Yep, but the hike back up will be tough. I don't think we should go that far."

"Daaad!" Her 10-year-old face turned thoughtful. "That's the next Rest House, right?" she said, nodding to it not far below.

"Yes, it's the Three Mile Rest House. Okay, maybe we can try it."

It had taken a lot of effort for Kathy to get pregnant with Jamie: Four failed in-vitro fertilizations, with me talking my wife into a fifth one-more-try IVF attempt. Each time, Kathy rushed my sperm in its sealed container to the fertility clinic, a half-hour drive over Mulholland. The clinic's walls were lined with photos of smiling couples and their babies.

Determination and crossed fingers can be required to create a family, especially if you wait until later in life. Kathy was turning 40, and I was in my early 50s. Fortunately, Warner Brothers, my employer at the time, had a generous health plan that covered the substantial cost of IVFs.

Jamie was born via caesarian in April of 2000. There was no problematic prematurity this time. She was such a good-sized to-term baby that she had to be pried out of the uterus by the doctor using a tongs-like device as I watched in the delivery room, joyful behind my surgical mask. Then, I cut an umbilical cord for the third time. The happy occasion was shared with some of the same medical team who had been through Josh's delivery, as well as Cassidy's. Kathy, worn out but otherwise fine, was released within 24 hours, holding a breastfeeding Jamie in her arms.

We had our family.

Back on that Bright Angel hike with Jamie, I'd soon stopped us again on our way down. I took in the steepness of the descent and imagined the climb back up.

"We really need to turn around now," I said, reluctantly playing the dad card and not leaving her a choice. She protested less this time, perhaps already feeling tired and realizing the truth of what I was saying. We turned around and began our hike back up.

I wished everything could stay the way it had been that day on a travel adventure with my 10-year-old daughter. There was an innocence to our days together that I didn't fully appreciate at the time—the special father-daughter bond that can exist and seems like it won't ever change.

My effortlessness on the hike back to the rim that day with Jamie encouraged me to take my cousin up on his offer to hike the Canyon with him and his pals, Rim to River and back in a day, which became the practice hike for my run.

Today, solo and trying to break six hours, there was no effortlessness. I needed to overcome whatever was going on with my body and persevere. The sun blazed down with gathering strength as I made my way upward. The effects of the rising temperature were exacerbated by my exertion, as I marshaled what was left of my energy.

A young online female fitness blogger had dubbed the upper reaches of the Bright Angel Trail ascent "The Death March." She nailed it.

I came around a switchback to find the Mile and a Half Rest House visible just up ahead. I changed back to a shuffle-jog, picking up my pace. Reaching the Rest House, I made it up to where several people were standing with their containers at the spigot and got in line. I poured out what was left of the warm water in the bottle I'd been carrying.

When it was my turn, I filled the bottle, retrieved one of the two remaining bottles from my daypack, emptied its lukewarm contents, refreshed it with cool water, and put it back in the daypack. Taking some sips from the bottle in my hand, I plodded up the curving stone steps that led up to the Rest House in order to get out of the sun.

The shelter was set into a hillside that was covered by brush and small trees. There were large cliffs rising behind the structure. Another of the oversized Canyon thermometers—the same as the ones at Indian Garden and at Phantom Ranch—hung above the entrance: 84 degrees. Next to the thermometer, a sign said, "EMERGENCY PHONE." Past the shelter were the bathrooms in a brown wooden structure containing pit toilets. I didn't need to relieve myself, not even for a pee, much less a bowel movement.

I elected not to stick around. I needed to get moving. I returned down the steps to get back on the Bright Angel, where I promptly stumbled over a rock and regained my balance.

"Hey, dude. Gotta watch that first step." I glanced down the trail and saw Eduardo coming up, followed by ASU Guy, with Bernardo and Francisco. I gave them a wave, but I didn't wait for them.

#EX-STUDENT REVOLUTIONARY:
"SMASH THE FASCIST STATE?"

One day in September of 1999, I testified before a California state commission hearing on media on-air diversity, which was headed up by Lieutenant Governor Cruz Bustamante. As I spoke about television progress in minority and gay and lesbian portrayals, I saw Tom Hayden slip into the room. The SDS Port Huron Statement drafter, Chicago Seven defendant, and now California state legislator took a seat near the Lieutenant Governor and watched the proceedings, which were being held in Hayden's State Senate district.

The last time I'd seen Hayden, we were both out in front of the Department of Justice headquarters in Washington, D.C., along with 10,000 protesters during the May Day "Four Days of Rage" in 1971. This was the demonstration about which Attorney

General John Mitchell was famously quoted as saying, "It looks like the Russian Revolution." The Justice Department protest was the climax of a series of actions against the Vietnam War that landed me in a jail cell with Abbie Hoffman three days earlier.

I recognized Abbie immediately from across the crowded cell, despite the gauze bandage that covered his nose and half his face. The face that was all over the media during the trial of the Chicago Seven. The face that adorned my copies of *Revolution for the Hell of It* and *Woodstock Nation*, amusing manifestos he authored that were de rigueur reading for the fun side of the Movement.

Abbie projected a certitude I could only envy, as if he never questioned himself. He would just flash that charismatic grin, carry on and get arrested, and it didn't faze him. As if he possessed none of the confusion and self-doubt that all too often plagued me.

I squeezed past the other prisoners, a dozen of us jammed into the cell.

"So, they got you too," I said.

"Hey, man, don't say anything. They don't know it's me."

"Right on," I said. "No problem."

I stared at the white surgical tape criss-crossed over Abbie's face. "What happened?" I asked.

"I took a two-by-four to some pigs. So they broke my nose."

"Wow," I said. "I put a boot to a motor-scooter cop and knocked him over. Made a run for it, but kind of hard to go too fast in these." I looked down at my steel-toed work boots, part of the uniform of the Weathermen, along with my Levi's, Sears work shirt, and denim jacket.

Abbie nodded and glanced warily around the cell block. He looked awfully somber for the leader of the fun side of revolution. There seemed to be a weariness about him. He wasn't smiling. Maybe it was because he'd been arrested one too many times.

Maybe it was because he was losing faith in revolution. Maybe it was because he was thirty-four to my twenty-two.

"Well, good luck," I offered. "I hope the cops don't figure out who you are."

"Yeah, man."

I returned to my spot as three men in suits—FBI, I guessed—walked along the row of crowded jail cells, pausing at each one, scanning faces. They stopped in front of ours and peered inside. I saw one of them point out Abbie to the others. I turned and glanced back. Abbie had the look of a caged animal.

A uniformed cop came into the corridor and announced anyone who would plead guilty to obstructing traffic could pay a ten-dollar fine and be set free. Since that meant the charge for me was obstructing traffic rather than what it could have been—assaulting a police officer—I considered myself lucky. I paid the fine and walked out the door, leaving Abbie and the rest of them behind.

Soon, I would completely abandon radical politics and its descent into violence and nihilism, including bombings, as I stepped back from the brink.

I continued to speak to the commission, fielding a question from a female member who asked about lesbian portrayals. I gave examples of progress, including *Serving in Silence: The Margarethe Cammermeyer Story*, which aired on NBC in 1995 and starred Oscar-winning actress Glenn Close. The movie told the story of army colonel Greta Cammermeyer, who'd been forced out of the Washington State National Guard for being gay. The film also featured the first bona fide lesbian kiss on broadcast television—which I'd advocated to allow. I also acknowledged to the woman on the panel, "Yes, there remains more to do."

I felt good about being able to bridge the gulf between Hollywood and the committed activists from a variety of advocacy groups represented in the room. It was hard to ignore the role of the 1960s civil rights and liberation movements—Black, Latino, gay and lesbian, etc.—and how they impacted what was now seen on television, as well as propelling my own advocacy for change in the medium. In that moment, I felt like the confounding political and counterculture twists and turns of my life finally tied together and made some sort of sense.

When the hearing ended, I walked over to Tom Hayden as he stood tieless in a sports jacket and chatting with the Lieutenant Governor. At least Hayden was still with us. So many weren't. Abbie Hoffman had disappeared underground in 1974 while out on bail in the wake of what he said was a police frame-up cocaine bust. In 1980, he revealed that he had been hiding in plain sight in upstate New York as environmental activist Barry Freed. In newspaper photos, Hoffman looked like an entirely different version of himself. The young, charismatic revolutionary I'd admired had given way to a middle-aged man with a thick nose (courtesy of plastic surgery to disguise his appearance), his turbulent hair cut short and a beard softening the strength of his jawline. At age 44, he looked like he could be a college professor, a psychologist, or your local rabbi. Hoffman received a one-year prison sentence and was released after serving four months. By 1989, he was living alone, took 150 Phenobarbitals with a bottle of Scotch, and lay down to die. His brother wrote a biography and revealed that Abbie was bipolar, explaining both his fearless charismatic leadership and his suicide.

Jerry Rubin was gone as well. I thought of him as Robin to Abbie's Batman in those halcyon revolutionary days. I'd asked him what we should do next when we were outside agitators at that New Jersey campus in 1969, and his response was, "I dunno, man. I did a hit of mescaline." After moving to Los Angeles and becoming a successful businessman (and a Yuppie rather than a

Yippie), Rubin died one day in 1994, hit by a car as he attempted to jaywalk busy Wilshire Boulevard.

I'd tried to make my own peace with one of the more troubling aspect of those days. On a business trip to Washington, D.C., I visited the Vietnam War Memorial for the first time. I stood before the flanged, black-marble wall covered with more than 58,000 names—the ones who went and served and died. I broke down before the power of that monument to the dead. The names inscripted on the wall included a fighter pilot who was a member of the wrestling team with me at Munich American High School in Germany. Shot down over Laos; dead at age 24.

The memorial visit didn't change my opposition to the war, but it brought up a major failing of the Movement at the time: too often demonizing those who went and served and dishonoring them when they returned.

"Excuse me," I said, as Hayden and the Lieutenant Governor were wrapping things up. I exchanged my own greetings with the Lieutenant Governor. He thanked me for coming—I was the only network television representative who would agree to appear before his commission and testify.

Before Hayden could move on, I introduced myself and shook his hand. Then I said, "You wouldn't guess it . . ." I indicated my tastefully pinstriped gray suit from Nordstrom's Hickey-Freeman Collection, my subdued bronze-colored Robert Talbott tie, and my polished cordovan Bass Weejuns dress loafers. ". . . but I used to be in SDS."

Tom Hayden looked me in the eye, slapped me hard on the shoulder with the heartiness of a politician, smiled and said, "Good man!"

CHAPTER 28

A CHARMED LIFE

I was breathing harder, sweat dripping down my forehead. I stopped, dropped the daypack beside me, took off my cap, and wiped my scalp with an arm. I had a view all the way to Indian Garden, which from here was a distant, lush green ribbon of trees surrounded by semi-arid landscape. Just to the left, I could see the Plateau Point Trail descending to where it met the Tonto Trail, which was visible as a winding strand heading west.

I couldn't help but note the irony of my choice of gear as I held the sweaty Phidippides cap in a hand. The running store it came from was named after the legendary Greek courier Pheidippides, although they changed the spelling of his name. He was said to have run from the plains of Marathon to Athens in 490 BC to announce the Greek victory over the Persians in battle. (His run gave the distance event, the marathon, its name when the modern Olympics were born in 1896). That part of the story was inspiring, but Pheidippides then collapsed and *died* after delivering the news.

I'd given Kathy my Facebook password, so she would be able to post the news of my death, whether today in the Canyon or some other time. I'd done it the previous year after the passing of a friend of mine from Munich American High School. He'd been a popular athlete and class president and had tracked me down online a few years ago. We'd spoken by phone, bonding over shared if somewhat different cardiac histories. His included open-heart surgery. A year and a half ago, I'd failed to take him up on his suggestion that I visit him in Palm Desert when he stayed there overnight on a trip. The two-hour drive from L.A. seemed like a hassle at the time and difficult to fit into my schedule. Besides, he and I had plans to get together in person at an upcoming high-school reunion in Munich during the summer of 2011.

Instead, there had been a Facebook post by his daughter that announced his death six months before the reunion. Shocked and filled with regret at not making the effort to see him in Palm Desert when I had the chance, I took a flight to attend his memorial service. The laudatory remarks about him included testimonies from people he'd helped in a drug-rehab program after recovering from his own addiction issues that were brought on by a failed attempt to become a professional baseball player following college pitching stardom.

I wished I'd known him through those years. The heartfelt comments at the memorial service were profoundly moving, and they made me wonder what would be said about me after I was gone. I couldn't see someone talking about what a great human being I was—that I'd done something as selfless and noble as my high school friend: reaching out to the drug addicted, bringing them into his home as part of their rehabilitation, touching and changing their lives.

What had I done like that? What had I accomplished of value and worth should I die soon—even today in the Canyon? Was I living a life I was proud of? That would take some thought. And if I *wasn't* living a life that I was proud of, what was the solution? Was change even possible at this point.

A CHARMED LIFE

Perhaps all things considered, I'd led a charmed life. Especially given my cardiac history and its miraculous—so far anyway—outcome. I had faced adversity and emerged relatively unscathed. Except for Josh. That was adversity in spades.

Within a few years following Josh's death, I lost the willingness to re-experience the tragedy with Kathy on his birthday and again, eight months later, on the anniversary of his death. The pain of reliving it was too great a burden—turning the pages of his photo album and the memory book as Kathy and I sat on the couch together, tears flowing. Selflessness was difficult to summon from within me. Instead of dodging the pain, I should have been willing to continue supporting Kathy through the yearly rituals. For her, it was a cathartic experience dedicated to preserving Josh's memory as she re-experienced her grief, her love, and the emotional tenacity of her caring for him—our lost but not forgotten first child.

"Are you alright?" a female voice was saying.

I opened my eyes. Standing before me, a lanky, uniformed woman came into focus. I took her to be a park ranger.

"Yes. Why?" I said, leaning against the wall of rock on the shade side of the trail.

"You look awfully pale. Do you have enough water?"

"Yeah. It's just a tough climb out." I stepped away from the rock, taking a swig of water for her benefit, and because I was also finally feeling thirsty.

"Okay," she said, eyeing me as if unconvinced. I became aware of a similarly uniformed male standing a few feet behind her. Two hatless teen girls came down the trail towards us.

They wore shorts, T-shirts, and flip-flops, and had a single bottled water between them.

"Excuse me," I heard the guy say to the girls. "We strongly recommend you turn around at the Mile and a Half Rest House." He pointed to it below. "You can refill that water bottle there first."

"Really?" said one of the girls.

"Honey, the hike back up will be a lot tougher than you think," said the woman ranger, "and it's only getting hotter." The girls looked at each other. "Damn," said the second one. "Is that, like, an order?"

"Sweetheart, we can't make you turn around. But we'd hate to have to use a helicopter to medevac you to the hospital in Flagstaff. I'm sure your parents wouldn't be happy about that."

"Okay," said the first girl. "Crap. We'll get some water and turn around."

They headed for the Rest House. So did the two rangers who I expected would post themselves there and try to dissuade other ill-prepared day hikers from going any further.

View of Bright Angel Trail coming up from Indian Garden

     RICK MATER

I grabbed my daypack, slung it from a shoulder by a single strap, stepped out onto the trail, and started to slow jog. After maybe a hundred yards, I switched to hiking.

The South Rim was tantalizingly closer. It was still impossible to identify anything beyond the rocky spires arising from the Kaibab Limestone. The human structures—the El Tovar Hotel, the Bright Angel Lodge, and the string of small tourist businesses along the rim—had been constructed just far enough from the edge that they didn't spoil the pristine view when looking up from down in the Canyon. Even the Kolb Brothers Studio on its perch, seemingly hanging over the edge when you were there in person, was invisible to me now.

STRAWBERRY POINT

It seemed like only yesterday I was hunting young lobsters with ten-year-old Cassidy and six-year-old Jamie at Strawberry Point in Kennebunkport. Walking out at low tide, the three of us approaching the tidal pools on the ocean side of the point—a narrow spit of land that disappeared almost entirely at high tide—where the young lobsters were dug in under their rocks.

The rocks needed to be lifted carefully to avoid injury to the creatures that were four or five inches in length and iridescent under the water. Then came the spirited fun of doing battle with them in their fighting stance: claws raised, giving quick nips to fingers—not painful but startling—as they moved backward to escape.

I caught one with a quick move of my own as Cassidy held the rock up and Jamie looked on. I grasped it by the thorax at the base of the tail where the claws had trouble reaching me. Ranger Rick in action, lifting the young lobster out of the water; it immediately went limp in my hand. Following those frantic machinations to escape, it stayed completely still with air surrounding it in place of ocean. Only its antennae moved slightly, and its carapace was now brown without the magic of its underwater iridescence.

There were a few minutes of close examination, the girls taking turns touching the creature. Next, we returned it to the water, shepherding it back under its rock so it could avoid the attacks of marauding seagulls. Then, the girls caught their own lobsters, laughing and crying out with delight.

It was strange to be in the Canyon today, separated from my daughters and my late-in-life identity as a father. Parenthood, which I avoided until I was well into my mid-40s, now felt *essential*. Without it, I was in danger of being adrift like I used to be before marriage, and even more self-involved than I feared I already was. I knew that when I returned from the Canyon, I should take a more dedicated, selfless, active role as their father, advisor, and hopefully, their confidante.

I thought about the Old Desert Fox Woman on the Great Arc. How she'd told me, "With age comes wisdom, don't they say?"

My own wisdom seemed long in coming, with no certitude that it would arrive at all.

I rested on a boulder in the shade provided by the rock wall on the inside of the trail, my daypack beside me. My socks and shoes were full of the red dust that began collecting while I descended the Great Arc.

Eduardo came hiking up towards me, along with ASU Guy, Bernardo, and Francisco.

"Hey, you're slowing down," Eduardo said. "You look wasted, man."

"Yeah, well, shit happens."

ASU Guy broke off and stood near me in what was left of a strip of shade on the uphill side of the trail. He drank some water from the bottle I'd given them. Maybe he'd re-filled it back at the Mile and a Half Rest House. His cap was sweat-stained, and he'd turned it around rapper style—which didn't make a lot of sense when it came to shielding your face from the Canyon sun. I watched Eduardo nurse some water from the purple container. Bernardo and Francisco joined us, both of them breathing hard, the quartet's smiles and youthful exuberance at the mouth of the Black Bridge tunnel a distant memory.

"How's your time goal going?" said Francisco.

"Not sure. I lost my running watch on a workout a few weeks ago and didn't bother to replace it." I held up my bare wrist.

"My phone might have a signal up this close," Bernardo said. He retrieved it from the small daypack around his waist. I watched, skeptically as he held the phone up, moved it around in the air, then stepped out into the middle of the trail away from the rock face. "Yep, a signal. It's 11:13."

"Wow, that makes it tough," I said.

"Of course it's tough," ASU Guy said, and he indicated the steepness of the trail with a nod.

"To break six hours, I mean."

"Isn't it just enough that you're doing this in the first place?" Eduardo said. "I saw you ahead of us a while back, and you were fucking running it."

"Well, yeah, I guess. I'm not supposed to be doing this to begin with."

"Why not?"

"I have four stents in an artery."

They appeared uncertain at how to respond to the revelation.

"I had a heart attack. It should have killed me. So, doing this in the first place is kind of a big deal. If I make my time goal, it's icing on the cake."

A lizard darted across a nearby rock.

"Dude, I got news for you," said Eduardo, wiping the sweat from his face. "The icing is fucking melting." He took another drink from the purple container as ASU Guy laughed.

A couple people breezily strolled down past us, followed by others in twos and threes.

"Okay, we're heading out," Eduardo said, and the four of them got up.

"Maybe see you in a bit," I said, taking a sip of water.

CHAPTER 29

SCALING THE MONSTER

My legs felt like lead, but the rest of me wasn't feeling right either. Running, no matter how slowly, was off the table. I was having trouble even thinking straight. I could see the final giant switchback above me, at the end of a long, incredibly steep climb. The one the young online female fitness blogger had dubbed "The Death March." I'd taken to calling it "The Monster." After the Monster came the last of the route, up through the lower and upper rock tunnels to the rim.

The angle here on the Bright Angel was a 38% grade versus the maximum of 18% on the South Kaibab. And it came at the worst possible time—at the very end. My energy was completely sapped. It was as if every cell in my body was screaming out in agony. What the hell was going on? The further up I went, the heavier my daypack became. I should have left my BlackBerry behind at the hotel room. Even that incremental weight now felt like a mistake. My smaller, lighter flip-cell would take care of my call to Kathy at the rim. I was glad I'd given that bottled water to Eduardo; now, I paused and emptied one from my daypack into the arid dirt alongside the trail. It felt like a sacrilege.

As I headed up the Monster, the trail opened up out over the Canyon—the vistas irrelevant to me at this point. I crossed a rock water break, forcing myself to lift my feet to clear it, only to be confronted with another ladder of rutted cross-trail logs.

I still had a shot at breaking six hours, but I could feel it slipping away. And I was growing wary. I'd made it almost all of the way out of the Canyon. Only the hardest mile of all remained. The sun was unrelenting, the ascent brutal. I began to have a real concern about stroking out, Kathy's words staying with me. Would the exertion trigger something—plaque ripping loose, a heart attack, a stroke—perhaps fatal this time?

Why was I doing this in the first place, I wondered? Why would I risk never seeing the girls again? What was I trying to prove? Did I know the reason? *The real reason?* Some of it was obvious. With my running distances limited by my cardiologist and marathons off the table—and my desire to attempt another one gone anyway—the Grand Canyon presented a unique challenge. One that didn't involve chasing some past race time I could never hope to match. Doing the Grand Canyon was appealing to me precisely because it *wasn't* running another marathon or half-marathon or trying to speed through a 5K or 10K. I knew any 5K faster than my 24:20 in 2008 was unlikely. My 5K PR of 18 minutes and change, achieved during my brief return to running in my 30s, was far out of reach.

I'd told myself that today was also about overcoming the odds and fighting the aging process and its inevitable decline. Finding something to do at age 64 that made me feel vital, engaged, and challenged—not throwing in the towel, even after my heart attack. Or maybe *especially* because of my heart attack, along with the two angioplasties, the four stents placed.

Doing the Canyon was an act of *defiance*. I chose to ignore doctors' warnings and overcome limited expectations in the wake of

View of the Bright Angel Trail and the North Rim

my cardiac issues. I was separating myself from the rest of them who were my age, the ones with their bad knees, couch potato ways, and sometimes bulging bellies. Those who were giving into aging and physical decline without a fight.

I wasn't going to disappear into retirement—from running or my job—unless at some point I changed my mind on my own timetable. Or else if I was confronted by some immoveable obstacle: a major injury, for example. Even then, I envisioned that I would segue to hiking if I wasn't running. A lot of hiking. Over hills and mountains. Endurance hikes combined with enjoying nature and exploration.

When I got as far as seriously considering a location for my later life after my TV job, once the kids left home, after the handiness of urban centrality, I had the thought that I could be living in Marin, across the Golden Gate Bridge from San Francisco. There I enjoyed getaways from L.A.—sometimes with Kathy and the girls, sometimes alone. Running up Mount Tam on Sunday mornings, enjoying the Redwood environs, the mountain trails, the gorgeous vistas, the quiet solitude. Challenging my body, the endorphin rush from my long run propelling what was for me the best day of the week.

I liked the notion of a fit and happy me thriving in some workable fashion as I aged. Becoming comfortable with what the next stage of my life would entail. Writing perhaps. My novel *Beat* finished, its sequel in the works, and more.

The girls would be off leading their own lives, although Jamie wasn't due to begin college until the year I turned 70. That was sobering. I was certainly in no rush to retire. And ongoing family responsibilities—paying for the girls' higher education—felt more like a source of comfort and an *anchor* for me than a burden.

Besides, my self-image—indeed, my *identity*—was wrapped up in my job and being the guy turning 65 who *wasn't* retiring. What was that all about? *Who was I if you stripped away the artifice of job-based identity?* That it assured me standing in society, especially given my shiftless days, part-time employment, and poverty in my 20s? The years spent finding accommodation with my personal ideals and a job that eventually worked for me. Or worked well enough. How would I face life—face myself—without the job-related routines and their imposed sense of order, structure, teamwork, and *purpose*. And without the kids after Cassidy and Jamie moved on? Empty nest syndrome wasn't a gender-defined condition.

I had no desire to return to those earlier, directionless times in my life in some new variation labelled "retirement." But at some point, it was inevitable that I would need to face that who-was-I question once and for all—whenever I retired, or the company retired me . . . unless I died first.

I stopped again and leaned against another rock in a sliver of shade. I dropped my daypack. I thought how it wasn't worth it to push myself past the limits of endurance and trigger something horrific—having made it through the heart attack and the two angioplasties and four stents, only to blow it on this self-administered ordeal. I just wanted to finish in one piece, to make it up to the rim without stroking out. Survive and reunite with the family.

I didn't care anymore if I broke six hours.

CHAPTER 30

PANGAEA ULTIMA

Eduardo was in front of me, along with his three companions. I'd caught them again—and it didn't matter. We hiked up together, all five of us silent, with only the sound of our shoes scuffling against the dirt and the rocks. Eduardo was off my left shoulder, ASU Guy and Bernardo right behind us, Francisco bringing up the rear. Soon, Eduardo and the others paused and took shelter in a bit of remaining shade on the uphill side of the trail.

"We don't have a crazy time goal," he muttered to me as I kept going. Leaving them behind I came up the final switchback of the Monster. The Bright Angel changed color here, shifting from reddish to the white-gray dirt of Kaibab Limestone. I remembered I was traversing what had once been Pangaea a couple hundred million years ago. Pangaea wasn't the final supercontinent, just the most recent. The movement of the landmasses around Earth on their tectonic plates never stops. The Pacific Plate under the western part of California, including Los Angeles, grinds past the North American Plate with the rest of California and the continental U.S., at a rate of about two inches a year, heading northwest as it slides along the San Andreas Fault. The North American Plate moves in the opposite direction.

One day, California and the bulk of the West Coast will break off completely, continuing to move northwest until it eventually slams into Japan. Meanwhile, South America will move east and wrap itself around Africa as the two continents—which split apart in the demise of Pangaea—are reunited. In the process, the Atlantic Ocean will close up; the Mediterranean will disappear as Africa rams into Europe; and the Indian Ocean will shrink as Australia heads north and collides with Southeast Asia.

In 250 million years, the various continents will have completed the process of converging to form the next supercontinent, which some scientists already have named: Pangaea Ultima.

The Grand Canyon will be long gone by then.

If Pangaea was the birthplace of mammals and therefore man, what would Pangaea Ultima bring? Perhaps mankind's demise during the long, slow ripping-apart of current landmasses, with climate change as oceans come and go, air and sea currents altering, mountains eroding and new ones forming in a slow-motion rollout of unimaginable turmoil and destruction. Or would our end come much earlier via nuclear war, global warming, an asteroid collision, or some other calamity, millions of years before Pangaea Ultima's creation?

I trudged up the last of the Monster in ongoing agony. I saw the Lower Tunnel just ahead. Cut through a rock formation that arched over the trail, it was part of the extensive work done to expand and improve the old Native American route to Indian Garden. The original trail had been an even steeper and more direct way up. There had been no giant final switchback, just a sheer, rocky climb.

Travel through the lower tunnel was quick, as I covered the dozen or so feet of its length. There were more tourists here. Day hikers passing me on their way down and seemingly without a care in the world, most without water. Some spoke English; the rest talked in foreign languages: French, German, Spanish, and more as they went by.

To my right and up above were Native American hieroglyphs drawn on the walls of the Canyon as far back as a thousand years ago: images of animals, hunting, and farming. Honey and I had spotted them as we hiked partway down the trail almost 40 years ago, and I'd pointed them out to Jamie on our own hike.

The Upper Tunnel lay just ahead. The short passageway was cut through a formation that extended out over the Canyon and ended after 30 or 40 feet with an abrupt drop to a rock outcropping. Just before the tunnel, a yellow diamond-shaped sign was posted—"DO NOT ENTER - DANGEROUS OVERLOOK"—that warned of going to the outcropping and the precipitous ledge that led there.

As I passed the sign, I observed a couple of young guys and a girl on the outcropping, taking photos and clowning around. Youth had its pros and cons. I doubted they knew that *Death in Grand Canyon* told the story of a 28-year-old Czech visitor who, ten years earlier, had also ignored the sign and gone out and posed for a photo—only to lose his balance and fall to his death.

On the other side of the tunnel, I picked up speed like at the end of a race, the "finish line" just up ahead—even throwing in a last half-assed attempt at a jog. This was it. There was no sense of triumph, only a grimaced "It's finally over." The Kolb Brothers Studio appeared on my left as the trail veered right for the final hundred yards or so, which was paved.

I felt like an alien as I emerged from the Canyon onto the blacktop of the rim path with Buckey O'Neill's cabin off to my left, now a part of the Bright Angel Lodge. I was an outlier in my state, surrounded by scores of tourists milling about in the heat of the day, taking photos of the view, as the voices of children filled the air with their excited chatter.

I put down my daypack and pulled out my BlackBerry. The time was 12:25 PM. I'd done the Canyon in six hours and 40 minutes. I regretted missing my time goal but was relieved to be finished without suffering some catastrophic medical emergency—chiefly that stroke Kathy was worried about. I wanted to call her and let her know I was back on the rim, but I was in no shape to do so without sounding like something was amiss.

I needed to get a shuttle back to the Visitor Center parking lot to retrieve my car, take a shower, and get it together before I called her. I wished I was staying at Maswick Lodge, like on my visit two years earlier with Jamie. I would just walk the few hundred yards from here. I would fall onto the bed for a few minutes, and after some rest, pull off my old running shoes, the red-dust encrusted socks, my Coolibar top, drop the old khaki shorts, and strip for a shower. But the Maswick had been booked up, my decision to choose this specific date spontaneous and at the start of tourist season.

I jammed the BlackBerry back into the daypack, zipped up the pocket, and made my way to the shuttle stop on the rim road. I stood among some people who were waiting there with no bus in sight. Each moment in line was an eternity. I had to suffer through the false alarm of a bus approaching, only to discover it was the Red Line and heading out to Hermit's Rest—the opposite direction of my destination.

I poked my head inside as the last of the people finished boarding.

"Do you know when the next Blue Line is?"

The driver said, "Should be five minutes behind me."

After what felt like forever, the Blue Line shuttle arrived. I climbed in and collapsed onto a seat, hunched over my daypack. Fortunately, no one took the space beside me. The last thing I wanted was to have to converse with anyone or even experience them close to me.

Bright sunlight flooded through the window. I closed my eyes. I had an urge to lie down in the aisle and go to sleep on the floor. The bus chugged along its circuitous route, first turning up the road to stop in front of the Maswick—which only tormented me with how much I wished I was staying there.

Cravings. I was having cravings.

God, I would kill for Gatorade. And potato chips. Yes, I had to have potato chips. I could taste them, crunchy and salty and so delicious. Should I hop off the shuttle when it reached the Market Plaza stop at the Canyon Village supermarket? No, I needed to deal with getting my car first, which was a stop after the store; then, I'd drive back to the market.

Finally, the shuttle pulled into the Visitor Center parking lot. I disembarked back where my day at the Canyon had begun. It could be hard to find my vehicle in the huge lot, now full of cars, RVs, and tour busses. It was a Saturday in June, after all, and now afternoon, so I was glad I'd had the presence of mind to park in the outer ring of spaces.

I retraced my steps around the perimeter. Thankfully, despite barely being able to think straight, I found my car quickly. I retrieved my keys from the daypack's little zip-up pocket, unlocked the trunk, threw my daypack inside, and snagged my wallet. Then, I got behind the wheel. I skipped retrieving the sunglasses from the visor, as I squinted into the sun. Concentrating hard to stay alert and focused, I drove to the parking lot exit, sitting erect and taut, my hands gripping the top of the steering wheel. I hung a right and headed back to the Canyon Village supermarket, barely keeping to the speed limit.

I parked and hopped out, striding past some metal tables and chairs for eating outside, and entered the store. Once inside, I grabbed a fruit punch Gatorade and a bag of Lay's potato chips. There was one person in front of me at each of the checkout lines.

　　　　RICK MATER

I chose a register, twisted off the top of the Gatorade, and chugged half the bottle as I waited. Then, I snagged some M&Ms from a rack beside me. The customer in front of me picked up their shopping bag and moved on as I set my stuff down on the rubber conveyer.

The checkout girl looked at me as she rang up the items. She glowed in the way 20-somethings do, simply because they're blessed with the gift of youth: skin smooth, hair not yet gray, body not yet betraying them. Her nametag read "Sue."

"Be right back," I said to her. "Give me just a sec." I went to the drink section, grabbed another Gatorade, and returned.

"In the Canyon?" Sue said, taking me in as she rang up the new bottle.

"Yep."

"Did you hike and go camping?"

"Actually, I ran it—to Phantom Ranch and back up. Well, mostly ran it."

"Never been down," she said.

"That's . . . interesting." Wow, how could you work at the Grand Canyon and never go down? I gave her the emergency $20 bill from my pocket.

"Bag?"

"Sure."

She handed me my change and a receipt as she placed the second Gatorade in the bag along with the half-empty bottle, the Lay's, and the M&M's.

Outside, I found a seat at one of the tables out front, ripped open the bag of chips with my teeth, not caring if some spilled, and began wolfing them down. Potato chips never tasted so good. I went through the entire package and finished off the first Gatorade. Before I started on the second, I tore into the bag of M&M's and ate the colorful chocolate candy in a few handfuls.

The change was palpable and immediate. I started to feel human.

Something about this was familiar, the excruciating combination of physical and psychological toll, the hard-to-pin-down cause of it, the near-failure to be able hold it together. The now-surprisingly fast improvement.

Electrolytes! *Goddamn Electrolytes!*

Jesus. Unbelievable. I'd repeated my rookie mistake from the Culver City Marathon almost 30 years earlier: not taking in enough water until it was too late, and more importantly, no snacks or power gels during the run.

It was time to call Kathy. I dialed the phone number for the house on my cell, hoping I'd get one of the girls picking up first and have a chance to chat for a minute.

"Hello," Kathy said.

"Hi, babe."

"Is everything okay?" She said it quickly, apprehension in her voice.

"Yes. I'm out of the Canyon. I'm going back to the Holiday Inn for a shower."

"Are you sure everything's okay."

"Yes. Everything's fine."

"I don't know why you had to put us through this, I wish—"

Despite her annoyance, it was good to hear her voice, to sense her concern, to have someplace to go to after today. Someplace where I belonged.

"Please tell the girls," I said, interrupting. "Are they around?"

"Cass is out. Jamie is doing homework. Why?"

"Well, never mind. See you tomorrow."

I drove to the hotel, passing the cars lined up to go into the park at the entrance. Entering my room, I finished off most of the second Gatorade, kicked off my shoes, stripped, and got into the shower. I decided to shave again as I debated whether I should just hit the road. If so, I wanted to look presentable by the time I reached L.A. I was originally going to drive back the next day, but now I wondered why I should stay. I wasn't even at lodging inside the park. There was no cousin and his pals to share breakfast with at the El Tovar the next morning, like we'd done on my practice hike. And I wanted to re-unite with the family—experience them around me, see the girls, be with Kathy.

I put on some clean underwear, shorts, and a T-shirt, and headed downstairs.

"Hey, I was thinking of checking out early." I said to the guy behind the counter.

The clerk glanced at his watch. He was in his 40s, I supposed, and had given me the recommendation for the Coronado Room restaurant the night before.

"Checkout was 11 AM," he said. "I can give you a pro-rated deal. Thirty dollars for the extra—let's call it three hours—if you're out by 2:30."

"That would be great. Thanks. I'll be back down in five minutes."

I took the elevator and packed my rollaway bag. The running shoes, red dust-covered socks, Coolibar T-shirt, and my Phidippides cap, along with the Asics stretch top, all got tossed into my *Buffy the Vampire Slayer* zip-up travel bag. I hung my daypack by a single strap over a shoulder. After a trip to the car, a quick heads-up phone call to Kathy, and a stop by the clerk again to settle up, I was gone.

CHAPTER 31

EPILOGUE— APRIL 11, 2021

I came running down the Ridge Trail in Los Angeles on my Sunday morning long run, the route twisted and rutted, with exposed roots, rocks, and loose stones that challenged my footing. I wore a red Grizzly Peak Half-Marathon T-shirt, running shorts, and a Phidippides cap as I ran. A face mask dangled around my neck, ready for me to pull it up as a courtesy if I encountered anyone.

We had lost a family member to the pandemic. In 2017, my younger brother Gene and I talked our father into moving to assisted living on the East Coast, only for him to die there after a bout with Covid three years later. He wasn't intubated in the end and died peacefully, appearing as if asleep, in September of 2020. Gene was there on the last day, and he texted me an emotional final photo showing him holding our father's hand. I was grateful that I had some enjoyable times and good conversations with my father in the years preceding his death. We had made our bigger peace with each other many years earlier. He enjoyed visits with us on family vacations in Kennebunkport and also coming to Los Angeles to see his granddaughters.

On my run today, a MedicAlert I.D. bracelet hung around my left wrist, with an inch-long inscribed brass insert:

DEFIBRILLATOR
CORONARY STENTS
NO MORPHINE, VICODIN

The defibrillator was implanted in the left side of my chest, the result of a cardiac event in 2016. I'd been working on my laptop while seated at a table in Peet's Coffee on Ventura Boulevard, pausing on my way home from my office at Lifetime. My heart suddenly seemed like it was speeding up, as if in some strange reaction to the cappuccino I'd just begun to sip. I blacked out and collapsed off my chair. My head smashed against the tile floor, and I came to immediately—the blow likely responsible for ending the cardiac event, which without interruption would have been fatal.

People rushed over.

"Are you okay?" a guy asked.

I struggled to sit up, everything confusing.

"Somebody grab some paper napkins," the guy said. Seconds later, he was wiping away blood from my forehead.

"Should we call an ambulance?" the stranger asked.

"No, it's okay," I said.

I regained my chair, feeling embarrassed. The confusion was clearing as I recovered my wits. "My wife is an RN, and we live nearby," I said. "Let me try texting her."

Kathy responded immediately and came to pick me up. In a few minutes, I was at the house, sitting on the couch in the living room. Kathy was telling me that she wanted to call an ambulance. I said, "No." Jamie—now a 16-year-old junior in high school—walked in from her bedroom as I felt another cardiac event coming on. I tried say something.

"You're having another syncopal episode!" Kathy said. Then, to avoid me falling off the couch, she ordered, "Get down on the floor!"

I moved to the floor, where kneeling, I keeled over, my face red, eyes bulging. Kathy shook me, and I came out of it, having not completely lost consciousness this time.

"Now, we need to call an ambulance!" she said.

Still, I resisted. I'd never been in an ambulance and didn't want to start now. Soon, Kathy was driving me to the emergency room, Jamie riding along with us. It would get me to the hospital faster than waiting for an ambulance, anyway.

Upon arriving, Kathy navigated the crowded emergency reception area, talked to staff, and got me into a room. I stayed in the hospital for three nights and left with the defibrillator—a round metal device about four inches across and about a half an inch thick—inserted through an incision under my left armpit and placed up against my ribs. A wire ran up the front of my chest, just under the skin, to a spot next to my heart. I had been diagnosed with ventricular fibrillation, which causes the heart to launch into rapid, irregular, palpitations and fail to pump blood—with fatal results. The defibrillator would emit a powerful shock if my pulse jumped to above 200. Now, I had my own equivalent of shock paddles, the emergency medical remedy for an attack of ventricular fibrillation.

The brass insert on my MedicAlert bracelet also included an 800 number for EMT technicians or other emergency personnel to call for additional details of my medical history. The bracelet never left my wrist. Strapped next to it when I ran was a Velcro sport armband, which included my address and who to contact in the event of an emergency: Kathy, along with her cell phone number.

I still hadn't gotten around to changing the emergency contact information, no matter the divorce in 2018, the kids both having gone off to college, our home sold, me renting a small house not far away. Perhaps I should have done things differently when it came to the family and marriage, with better follow-through on my professed good intentions, including that day on the Grand Canyon run.

But life is about moving forward. Jamie came out as non-binary and is in their junior year of college, awarded a grant to do advanced research in their field of choice: psychology. My brother Gene embraced her gender truth as trans and is now my sister Jeanne. Cassidy pursues art, displays a passion for working with kids, and lives in Northern California. My novel *Beat* was finally finished, publication imminent.

I'm striving to find that path to the next stage of my life, as I navigate an uncertain future. So far anyway, I'm still employed full time in television. At least my Alzheimer's warning signs hadn't gotten much worse. I just needed to be extra careful and re-read every email and text, making any needed corrections before sending them.

My life now feels like it's about manifesting a meaningful present and not so much pondering a legacy. Am I living a life I'm proud of? I've had a lot of time to think about that in the past few years. I suppose there are parts of my life I'm proud of and things I'm not so proud of. I think that's probably true for most of us. Even my late friend from Munich American High School would likely have said that, especially about his drug-addicted younger days—before he turned everything around so selflessly at the end.

Through everything, my Sunday long run remains a loyal and constant ally. As I came running down the Ridge Trail today, I was surrounded by chest-high yellow wildflowers blooming from the winter rains, making for a sunny, double-sided, golden ridgeline. The flowers brushed up against me as I passed, leaving a light dusting of pollen on my clothes, my arms, my face.

I rounded the curve just before the weeping boughs of the lone pepper tree and reached the stretch where the route leveled off for several dozen yards. There were steep drops on both sides and lofty unobstructed views in all directions. I could see Fryman Canyon below to the right. Above it and across the way, a rustic stretch of Mulholland Drive, devoid of houses, wound against a brush and tree-filled hillside. On my left and to the north stood the Santa Susanna Mountains, and straight ahead to the east, the rugged Verdugo Hills. Mount Wilson rose in the distance, its 5,700-foot summit sometimes crowned with snow, depending on the season. Mount Baldy was visible beyond it, soaring over 10,000 feet and more often snow-capped.

I'd done some training on Mount Wilson—from the base to the summit and back down—for my return to the Grand Canyon to run it once more in 2013. I brought Gatorade with me to the Canyon this time and consumed it, along with power bars and sports gel, during my run. I broke six hours with a 5:54 time. Feeling awfully tired but otherwise okay, I walked the few hundred yards from the Bright Angel trailhead to shower in my room at the Maswick Lodge.

My time goal achieved, I switched to more Zen-like solo Canyon hikes going forward. Down the Grandview Trail for a hike to the Last Chance Mine at Horseshoe Mesa on the Tonto, where Margaret Bradley had embarked on her fatal run.

I did a subsequent springtime hike at dawn on a weekday, descending a South Kaibab Trail that was virtually devoid of people. When I reached the Tip Off, I cut west and traversed the Tonto Trail, stopping to visit a spring that was the source for Pipe Creek below in its ravine. There were tadpoles in a pool for me to enjoy, so I squatted and watched them for as long as I desired this time. It was just me and the Canyon's majestic solitude as the sun was coming up and radiating soft, early morning light. I stood

   RICK MATER

and gazed all round me. O'Neill Butte was above, just to the east. Higher still were Yavapai Point, Mather Point, and Yaki Point on the South Rim.

This was as close to a mystical experience as I could imagine. Alone on the Tonto, surrounded by the grandeur of the Grand Canyon at daybreak, the North Rim towering on the other side of the Colorado River gorge, with its own ravines, buttes, and points, along with its fancifully monikered, mountainous temples—Isis, Osiris, Shiva, and Vishnu, plus the Tower of Ra.

Leisurely, I hiked the Tonto. I was in no rush to surrender the solitude. Instead, I wandered off the narrow trail to explore the surrounding terrain: the spring and its pools, a nearby cluster of prickly pear cactus bursting with bright, lavender flowers.

Returning to the route, I continued along its meandering four and a half miles across the Tonto Platform to where the trail joined the Bright Angel below Indian Garden. And there I ascended.

Life is temporary and unpredictable, and the Universe can be an unkind and unforgiving place, but also one to be appreciated and lived in with gratitude while we inhabit these bodies, on this planet, in this solar system, circling this sun, in this particular galaxy.

Today, running high up on the Ridge Trail this sunny April morning, I passed through the golden path of wildflowers. As I reached the dirt straightaway after the lone pepper tree, I gave a triumphant fist pump and announced out loud, *"Look, Ma! I'm on top of the world! I love you!"* And then, after a few more strides, *"Seventy-three, four stents, a defibrillator in the side of my chest, and still at it!"*

ACKNOWLEDGMENTS

Thanks to: Freelance editor Annie Tucker for her work on an earlier draft of this book. Michael Snyder—culture blaster, journalist, broadcaster, and screenwriter—for his subsequent copy editing. My cousin James Mater for inviting me to hike the Grand Canyon with him and for providing some of the photos used in this book. Katherine Wing for reviewing portions of the manuscript to help ensure medical accuracy and for otherwise reading material which features her. And a shout out to the terrific team at Mayfly Design: Jess LaGreca, Julie Scheife, and Ryan Scheife.

The names of the doctors in the book have been fictionalized, as have the names of people I encountered in the Grand Canyon. At Jamie's request, I have used their self-selected first name in place of their birth name throughout.

Rick Mater
Los Angeles, California 2022

AUTHOR'S BIOGRAPHY

Rick Mater was born in Pinner, England, and grew up in California, New Jersey, and Munich, Germany. In high school, he ran the mile on the track team, and in college he lettered in cross country.

Distance running saved Mater's life. During a 2007 run, he was able to survive a heart attack brought on by a complete occlusion of the LAD (left anterior descending aorta). His survival was due to ancillary blood vessels created by his body in response to the rigors of distance running. This permitted enough blood to circulate around the LAD blockage and prevent a massive fatal heart attack. He has four stents in arteries and a defibrillator implanted in the side of his chest.

Mater lives in Los Angeles, where he has had a long career working in television. He was formerly married and has two 20-something children. He continues to run.

Website: Richardlewismater.com